Self-esteem

Self-esteem

A Guide for Teachers

David Miller and Teresa Moran

Los Angeles | London | New Delhi
Singapore | Washington DC

SAGE Publications Ltd
1 Oliver's Yard
55 City Road
London EC1Y 1SP

SAGE Publications Inc.
2455 Teller Road
Thousand Oaks, California 91320

SAGE Publications India Pvt Ltd
B 1/I 1 Mohan Cooperative Industrial Area
Mathura Road
New Delhi 110 044

SAGE Publications Asia-Pacific Pte Ltd
3 Church Street
#10-04 Samsung Hub
Singapore 049483

Library of Congress Control Number: 2011935881

British Library Cataloguing in Publication data
A catalogue record for this book is available from the British
Library

ISBN 978-0-85702-969-0
ISBN 978-0-85702-970-6 (pbk)

Typeset by Dorwyn, Wells, Somerset
Printed in Great Britain by MPG Books Group, Bodmin, Cornwall
Printed on paper from sustainable resources

Contents

About the Authors

David Miller is Professor of Primary Education at the University of Dundee. Before entering higher education he worked as a primary teacher in the UK and abroad, and latterly as Deputy Head of a large primary school. Much of his work in higher education involves research and teaching in the area of personal and social aspects of classroom life. He has worked extensively with undergraduate and postgraduate students and practising teachers, producing teaching materials, professional papers and CPD materials in this area, in addition to research articles. His doctoral thesis was entitled 'Peer learning and the duality of self-esteem'.

Teresa Moran is the Associate Dean (Education and Professional Development) at the University of Dundee. She has been a teacher educator for fifteen years, and for fourteen years prior to this she was a class teacher then a Deputy Head Teacher. The experience in the schools in which she worked was an excellent grounding for the work she has subsequently undertaken with student teachers and teachers. During her career in teacher education her main interest has been in the area of Religious and Moral Education, values in education and the pastoral care and well being of pupils. Alongside this has been her role of supporting students in developing their classroom practice, expertise and confidence in their ability.

Acknowledgements

The authors are grateful to Alan McLean and Dr Maureen Moran for helpful feedback on drafts. Special thanks go to Anne and Kirsty Miller for their careful proofreading and constructive feedback during the course of the writing.

1

What This Book is About

Introduction

In an article entitled 'Self-esteem: the kindly apocalypse', the writer (a philosopher) recalled a conference he had attended. At the end of the presentation, questions were invited from the audience:

> The speaker responded to the first question at the end by saying, 'That's a very fine question, a really interesting and important question'. It had seemed to me a fairly straightforward question, and I puzzled over why he thought it so significant. But this was intellectual energy wasted: every question, it turned out, was interesting, important, truly insightful or a question the speaker was enormously grateful had been asked. (Smith, 2002, pp. 92–3)

The writer went on to argue that this is a kind of dishonesty, albeit probably practised for benign reasons. Many who work in education will recognise the scenario, undoubtedly mirrored in countless classrooms and lecture theatres. Most will understand the reasons for the speaker's approach. It is possible that some may also share a sense of unease that there is something less than honest about this approach. If so, this book may help to overcome that sense of unease.

This book has been written for student teachers, their tutors and teachers in primary classrooms. However, as you read, it may become apparent that the main issues, the underlying theories, and many of the techniques described are relevant to those who work in other sectors too. In fact, having read this book, you may arrive at the conclusion that the material applies to individuals in many contexts, and at all stages of life. This is certainly the feedback we have had when presenting our work at conferences and in-service sessions.

Essentially, our aim is to provide advice about how to enhance the self-esteem of children. But it is not just a catalogue of tips for teachers to try out in their classes. Certainly, advice on strategies and techniques makes up a significant proportion of the content, but the book is about more than this. In order to intervene effectively in the classroom, theoretical under-standing is essential. It is difficult to see how someone can effectively enhance self-esteem in the classroom without a sound understanding of its fundamental structure, how it is influenced and why certain techniques are more likely than others to help children. Accordingly, the early chapters provide a summary and analysis of the key theoretical and empirical work in the area. This includes examining what we mean by self-esteem, explor-ing some basic theoretical ideas, and reflecting on the messages we may safely take from the research in this area. This process may encourage you to rethink some of your own attitudes – or it may reinforce your current beliefs. In either case, it should empower you to develop your practice with a clear sense of direction – and with increased confidence.

Why another book on self-esteem?

The fact that you are reading this presupposes that you have a particular interest in self-esteem – or a particular purpose behind learning about the key messages in the book. It may be that you have been asked to read it for some course work, or that you are looking to update your knowledge in this area. In terms of your own attitudes, you may be approaching the content firmly committed to the belief that self-esteem enhancement is an import-ant part of the teacher's role. But, equally, you may be flicking through the pages with a more sceptical eye; you may wonder what another book on this topic can add to an aspect of school life which already receives much attention. In terms of practice, you may be interested in adding to your repertoire of enhancement techniques – or you may be critical of what is currently being done in the name of self-esteem in schools. Of course, these last two perspectives are not mutually exclusive; one can be committed to enhancing self-esteem but at the same time hold reservations about some aspects of current practice. Whether one of these perspectives – or some other – reflects your own position, we believe there will be issues in here which will stimulate personal as well as professional reflection.

Indeed, one might reasonably ask, why do we need another book on the subject? We believe there are several good reasons. As we explain in more detail later, one reason is that much of what we believe about self-esteem is not supported by research evidence. To take just one such example: there is an assumption made by many teachers that improving the overall self-esteem of children results in academic gains. While many who read this may be able to provide examples of individual cases where this appeared to be true, the uncomfortable fact is that there is little 'hard' research evidence to support such a belief. Several comprehensive and well-respected reviews of the literature have arrived at this conclusion, and the message has been picked up by many who have subsequently used it (and misused it) for their own purposes. However, as in many areas of social research, the issues here are contested, and the picture is not a straightforward one. Although the links between *overall* self-esteem and school performance are neither strong nor consistent, there is clear evidence of a relationship between more *specific* aspects of self-esteem and the related areas of academic performance. As professionals, a challenge for us is to reconcile apparently conflicting messages and decide what the evidence really does tell us. Chapters 2, 3 and 4 should help in this process.

A second reason why a new book is necessary follows on from this point. There exist several different research paradigms in this area – that is, different ways of conceptualising and investigating self-esteem. The field is characterised by different groups of researchers investigating different aspects of self-perceptions, using different methods – and, it has to be acknowledged, rarely referring to the work of the other groups. Sometimes different writers use different terminology for what appears to be the same phenomenon; one example is the way in which self-concept and global self-esteem are seen to be synonymous by some writers. Others differentiate these terms – but not consistently. On the other hand, sometimes different writers use the same terms – but with different meanings – and this can be even more confusing. An important example here is the use of the term self-worth; some use it interchangeably with self-esteem, while for others (including ourselves) it has a more specific meaning.

So, the language is not always shared, and one does not have to read many texts in this area before a realisation dawns that the area of self-perception is complex. If the literature is not exactly disparate, it certainly lacks consensus in many key areas. So where does this leave the committed (but busy) teacher and student teacher, keen to make sense of the topic – and keen to make a difference in the classroom? Well, if some of the messages above may be perplexing, and even disheartening, there is good news to follow. There is one model of self-esteem which is gaining currency – and which has some important benefits to offer us. One of these benefits is that the model is capable of incorporating the main ideas of the key writers in this complex area; it does so in a convincing manner, and in a way which is able to explain previous research findings. What is more, the messages that emerge have particular relevance for teachers; they resonate with their experiences and seem intuitively 'right'. They also serve to direct classroom practice. This approach, known as a two-dimensional model of self-esteem, will be explained and analysed in some detail. It will be central to the strategies outlined in later chapters.

For a third reason, we might add the suspicion (let us call it no more than that) that some practices carried out in the name of self-esteem enhancement may be of doubtful value. There is a feeling in some quarters that certain techniques do little to develop genuine self-esteem, and indeed may have potentially undesirable consequences. Examples here include the emphasis on activities to make every child 'special', creating a no-blame culture, adhering to the principle that no one should be allowed to fail a task, and the over-use of praise. While such practices are frequently justified in relation to educational aims, some might not stand up to critical scrutiny. At the very least, it might be worth asking whether *in practice* there are some disadvantages to them.

Figure 1.1 'So, is there a problem?' Reproduced with permission from Lia Monforte, Fashionhut.net

The self-esteem backlash

There can be little doubt that such concerns have helped to fuel what has been called the self-esteem backlash. Several prominent academics, politicians and social commentators have attacked the emphasis on self-esteem enhancement in schools, and particularly what they see as frivolous or ill-advised practices. These criticisms will be examined in more detail later, but a key message from such writers is that our attempts to protect children from failure and make them 'special' are often at the expense of genuine learning and real personal growth. It is not difficult to appreciate the good intentions behind policies that try to ensure there is no failure in school: no wrong answers (no crosses or red pen), making everyone a winner, playing games on a no-score basis, and ensuring that at award ceremonies everyone gets a prize. However, it might be a mistake to ignore the possibility that such practices may also have a downside. According to some commentators, they may contribute to underachievement, a failure to cope with challenge and children who lack determination and resilience. We look in more detail at these issues in Chapter 4.

As the preceding paragraphs illustrate only too clearly, one of the most notable characteristics of the whole area of self-esteem is the polarisation of views. At the risk of resorting to caricatures, on the one hand we have those who see self-esteem as a panacea, who argue it is impossible to have too much self-esteem, and who would set it as the main purpose of education. On the other, we have the critics who assert that self-esteem policies have produced individuals who are boastful and self-obsessed; they are more likely to deny their faults, or make excuses for their poor performance and behaviour, than try to improve them. Thoughtful readers (including, we suspect, most experienced teachers) know that between these extremes there is an alternative perspective on self-esteem.

A positive but realistic perspective on self-esteem acknowledges that while there may be dangers with artificially inflated self-esteem, there are many more serious problems associated with low self-esteem. These problems influence children's learning but, equally importantly, they may have serious consequences for their personal and social lives. Although we have explained above that many beliefs in relation to self-esteem are contested, there is a general consensus that low-self-esteem individuals tend to underachieve, be more at risk from a range of social and personal ills and tend to live less fulfilling lives. We suspect many who enter the teaching profession need no more justification than this to target self-esteem as an educational goal.

However, the key point here is that the aim of a meaningful self-esteem enhancement programme is not to artificially inflate self-esteem with a range of superficially appealing techniques (often pedalled by those with a financial interest in so doing). Instead it is to use sound knowledge about the structure of self-esteem and the processes of enhancement to help children to develop a healthy and realistic sense of self. Stated simply, a healthy self-esteem involves recognition of our positive qualities and an acceptance of our less-positive ones. It is this perspective which guides what you will read in this book.

To conclude this section: if the landscape of self-esteem is both confused and confusing, where does this leave teachers who want to gain a clear picture in order to help their pupils? Well, despite the uncertainties and some unpromising messages that emerge in this area, the good news is that most caring teachers retain an interest in the self-esteem of their pupils. Their convictions, often formed in the light of experience, lead them to believe that in genuine self-esteem we have something important – something that is worth persevering with. We hope this book will help the reader to avoid the distortions produced by the wrong kind of emphasis on self-esteem, while giving them the knowledge they need to help develop in pupils a realistic and positive sense of self.

What then are the key ideas we work with?

We will start with the nature of self-esteem – its fundamental structure and how it is influenced by life experiences. In everyday language, we tend to share a common understanding about what we mean by self-esteem; however, when we come to define it, things are not so straightforward. In fact, despite being an enduring construct in psychological theory (for more than a century), the wide variety of definitions, models and measures highlights a lack of consensus amongst workers in the area. We examine some of these differing definitions and models, and show how an alternative model is capable of incorporating the differing perspectives and explaining the varying research findings in the field. That model emphasises that how we feel about ourselves involves two separate judgements: how worthwhile do I feel, and how competent am I to tackle the challenges I face? It is known as the two-dimensional model of self-esteem.

Since self-esteem is a dynamic construct, it is necessary to understand the processes involved in its formation and modification. We look at a series of questions in relation to this. What are the factors that influence a sense of self-worth? What sort of experiences help to create – or damage – self-competence? To what extent are these processes influenced by others? These are important questions which we need to answer if we are to understand the growth process. Of course, as teachers, a fundamental issue is what we can – and should – do to enhance the self-esteem of our pupils. Central to the discussion here will be the clear messages which emerge from the two-dimensional model of self-esteem. Viewing classroom interactions from this perspective provides us with a clear set of guiding principles, and helps to inform strategies and techniques.

As indicated above, some practices have developed in primary schools in the past in the name of self-esteem enhancement which many believe may be questioned. One of the reasons for this is that such self-esteem activities were seen as taking time away from the 'important' work of the classroom: learning in the core subjects. In contrast, many of the strategies we describe in the later chapters of this book allow teachers to enhance the self-esteem of children while at the same time improving their learning. That is, the techniques become part of the teacher's day-to-day teaching in the core subjects. One of the advantages of this approach is that it counters one of the key criticisms of the anti-self-esteem lobby; we show that self-esteem enhancement does not have to be at the expense of core learning. This perspective can help to narrow what has become known as the self-esteem divide: the gap that exists between those who see themselves as primarily responsible for teaching knowledge and skills, and those who see a broader role in terms of helping to support the personal and social development of the child. As should become clear as you read the book, many of the processes described have relevance to both groups of teachers.

It will be possible for those interested mainly in classroom techniques to start reading this book from Chapter 5 onwards, but we would encourage readers not to skip the theoretical sections in Chapters 2, 3 and 4. We say this for three reasons. First, it is generally accepted that knowledge of theory is important to help understanding, and move beyond the model of teacher as technician. In our pre-service work with teaching students and continuing professional development (CPD) work with experienced practitioners, we have witnessed many 'Aha!' moments, with individuals explaining that the theoretical ideas we described had helped them to understand the behaviour and mindsets of children (and other adults) they had met. Understanding and believing in the fundamental structure is an important step in developing classroom practice. Second, at a practical level, the theoretical understanding provides a lens through which to view classroom interactions.

In a contested and complex area, it provides a clear conceptual model which allows analysis of events, and points towards productive courses of action. It helps us to see the wood as well as the trees. And third, it allows extrapolation. Our list of techniques and strategies is not exhaustive, and understanding the main principles allows readers to develop ideas of their own, tailored to their own pupils in their own school contexts.

An overview of the chapters

Following this introduction, Chapter 2 will provide a general overview of research and theory in the area, and summarise the key messages that emerge. We look at the way in which self-esteem has been conceptualised, and in the process consider several other self-referent terms – many of which are used interchangeably. We provide an overview of the dominant approaches to the study of self-esteem: the unidimensional model, where self-esteem is primarily seen as an attitude towards the self, a development of this in the form of a multi-dimensional model and finally a more complex hierarchical model, which is based on a set of differentiated and hierarchical relationships. We shall look at some key messages from the literature in these areas. In the course of this chapter, we shall also look at the debate around what some writers call the contingencies of self-esteem. These are the factors on which we stake our self-esteem and, simply stated, if we value a particular characteristic, our self-judgements in that area become more important to our self-esteem. However, in contrast, some writers argue that this 'importance effect' is not significant in determining levels of self-esteem. Effectively, your performance affects your self-esteem, whether you care about it or not. As with many areas of self-esteem, there is significant disagreement here, and we will refer readers to the evidence that is available.

An important area to examine relates to the processes which impact upon our self-perceptions. This has particular relevance to teachers. In order to help others, we need to know how self-esteem 'works': the processes and experiences that determine our levels of self-esteem. Once again, there are many different perspectives in this area, but we describe four key processes which summarise the key influence on our self-perceptions.

In Chapter 3, the structure of the two-dimensional model of self-esteem will be described in more detail, and illustrated with examples of typical behaviours and mindsets. Once more, theoretical and empirical evidence to support this model will be examined. Links will be made with work in other areas, such as childhood resilience, and the chapter will conclude with a summary of the important messages for schools. In many ways, these are encapsulated in a key phrase in the literature: helping children to feel 'competent to cope, and worthy of happiness'.

In Chapter 4, we take issues arising from the theoretical material in Chapters 2 and 3 and relate these specifically to the classroom. After discussing the 'self-esteem debate' as it relates to education, we look at the research evidence related to school performance. This will cover several main issues. One is the relationship between global self-esteem and educational performance, which may appear disappointing to self-esteem enthusiasts. Another is the relationship between work in the area of academic self-concept and educational performance which, in contrast, is very encouraging. An important question for teachers relates to what psychologists call *ecological validity*: to what extent does the research conducted reflect the reality of classroom life?

Following on from this point, we then complement these perspectives with several recent studies which use a two-dimensional model of self-esteem to examine aspects of classroom interactions. From this analysis, we draw out a series of principles that will guide the later chapters, focusing on classroom practice. These principles will be used to revisit previous notions of 'good practice', and in so doing highlight those aspects to which we may have paid insufficient attention in the past. Developing a sense of self-competence will be central to this. Several key ideas will be introduced here, and links will be made with other aspects of personal and social theorising. We shall introduce some important ideas about motivational mindsets, focusing on the way in which individuals view their ability and their performance. The use and misuse of praise will also be discussed, including the dangers of what has been called 'non-contingent success' (that is, when learners receive feedback which is out of proportion to the achievement). The overall aim of this chapter is to equip the reader with a clear theoretical framework for the next four chapters, which relate to classroom techniques.

Chapters 5 and 6 focus on competence-based strategies. In the first of these, we look specifically at creating and recognising achievement. The notion of *creating* achievement may ring warning bells for some. They may (mistakenly) see vestiges of some questionable techniques: providing children with work that they can do comfortably, in order to ensure that they are protected from failure. But this is not what we are advocating. On the contrary, we do not believe that protecting children from failure is likely to enhance self-esteem. There are many reasons why we say this. Failure is part of life for all of us; learning to cope when we *do* fail is a necessary skill for life. It is certainly part of growing up, and protecting children from failure is hardly likely to develop resilient children who work to overcome difficulties when they encounter them. In relation to academic work, failure to grasp a new idea or master a new skill is an integral part of learning; the lessons learned from such failure can enhance the prospects for future success. The important point is this: it is not failure per se which harms self-esteem, but people's reactions to that failure. It is the way that the failure is interpreted, by the child and by significant others. One child may be criticised, punished or ridiculed for her failure; she will be disheartened and give up, and will be diminished personally by the experience. Another may be encouraged and supported to overcome the failure; she will be motivated to persevere and master the skill – and benefit accordingly. It is within these processes – not within the act of failure itself – that we see the links with self-esteem.

Chapter 5 will discuss classroom techniques which, on the basis of theoretical or empirical research, are likely to develop a sense of self-competence. The main themes here will include effective differentiation, creating tasks which allow a sense of control, the use of formative assessment techniques, the potential of game-based learning, the benefits of various forms of peer learning and the use of ICT. The aim will be to explain the processes, illustrate the theoretical links with some classroom examples, and provide further pointers for readers to follow up if they wish. Chapter 5 is complemented by Chapter 6, in which we continue the competence-building focus by looking at the way in which we can help children to develop positive mindsets. This involves looking at beliefs and attitudes which influence how children view their performance and make judgements about their ability. Key themes include changing children's views of ability, creating motivational mindsets, the use of contingent praise and teacher expectations.

Following on from the competence focus in Chapters 5 and 6, the following two chapters focus on worth-based strategies. As with the chapters on self-competence, the aim will be to explain the key elements with a few examples, and provide further pointers for follow up. In Chapter 7, we focus on the creation and maintenance of a worth-based ethos. An important aspect here is the provision of affirming messages about a child's intrinsic worth: the basic right of an individual to be respected as a person, irrespective of their abilities. Given the role of the primary teacher in the lives of young children, a key feature will be teacher modelling. Central to this chapter (as with those that precede it) is the complex issue of praise and we consider its advantages and disadvantages in relation to self-worth. We make a distinction between affirming messages and contingent praise, and focus on the importance of the former for enhancing feelings of worth. We also look at ways of incorporating pupil voice in the day-to-day life of the school and taking opportunities to investigate issues of concern to the children. Many teachers will be familiar with 'circle time' techniques, even if they are not aware of the paucity of research evidence in this area. The evidence here will be used to remind the reader once more of a fundamental tenet of our approach: when planning to nurture self-esteem, rather than thinking in terms of enhancing self-esteem per se, it is likely to be more productive to focus on developing one or other dimension of it – self-worth or self-competence.

In Chapter 8, we maintain the focus on self-worth, but look now at how conduct can influence feelings of worth. We consider this in two ways: through pro-social activities and in terms of general conduct in the class. In relation to the former, we look at 'required helpfulness', an idea borrowed from the literature on resilience, where children are placed in situations where others expect (and require) help from them. We look in some detail at one aspect of peer-assisted learning – peer tutoring – and in particular the messages which we can take from studies in this area in relation to self-esteem gains. These are related specifically to the way in which such tutoring is organised and managed, and the resultant effects on children's self-percep-tions. We consider the relationship between behaviour management techniques and beliefs about worth, and identify some key characteristics which teachers may focus on. We conclude this chapter by looking at ways in which we can maximise worth-enhancing opportunities within main-stream curriculum activities, illustrating the point with reference to Citizenship and Global Studies, philosophical thinking and Religious and Moral Education (RME).

We conclude with Chapter 9, which does three things. First, it recaps briefly on some key points, before considering issues which merit further attention. It finishes with two important messages. The first of these is that school attainment and self-esteem have often been placed in opposition to each other: competing demands on a teacher's time. The two-dimensional model, with its focus on self-competence, illustrates how both can be devel-oped simultaneously. Feelings of competence can only come from achievements which are real and meaningful – that is, acquiring new knowledge or mastering new skills – and then recognising that achievement. One consequence of this perspective is that both sides of the self-esteem divide can be brought together, and the debate in the area of self-perception can then move on in a more informed manner.

The second message is related to this – and sounds a note of caution. There is evidence that the self-competence dimension is now being recognised; this is undoubtedly a good thing. However, there are also signs that self-competence – in the form of its alter ego, self-efficacy – is being promoted as an *alternative* to self-esteem. While we share the enthusiasm for efficacy, from a self-esteem perspective it is only half of the picture. One of the criticisms that might legitimately be levelled at self-esteem enhancement programmes in the past was that they focused on only one dimension of self-esteem – in that case, the other dimension, self-worth. As will be evident to the reader by this point, this was unfortunate for several reasons – with both educational and personal consequences. We must ensure we do not repeat the mistakes of the past. If we accept that healthy self-esteem requires a focus on *both* worth and competence, a balanced approach is required. Certainly that is the message with which we leave the reader: when thinking about our self-esteem, and more broadly our mental health, competence and worth are entwined beyond separation.

2

An Overview of Self-Esteem Theory

> **Key ideas in this chapter**
>
> This chapter provides an overview of self-esteem theory and the research evidence which underpins it. The field is rich in terms of ideas, but this very richness can provide difficulties because of the wide range of perspectives adopted and the variation in terminology employed. You will learn about:
>
> - some key ideas which have influenced how we talk about and investigate self-perceptions
> - some issues surrounding the definition of terms
> - the main research paradigms in this area – that is, the main ways in which self-esteem has been investigated, and the beliefs that underpin these approaches
> - four key processes believed to influence our self-esteem.

Introduction

A concern with how people value themselves is hardly new. References to what we now call self-esteem can be found in the work of the ancient philosophers; for example, more than three hundred years before the birth of Christ, Aristotle made reference to the idea of self-respect[1]. However, there is little doubt that an interest in self-esteem has grown significantly in modern times. In particular, the last decades of the 20th century saw the emergence of what has been called the self-esteem movement. This is a general label which has been applied to the increase in interest and activity – both organisational and financial – in the area. The roots of this can be found in beliefs about the importance of self-esteem; that is, its importance to general psychological health and well-being. But alongside such beliefs, there are those who argue that a healthy self-esteem is related to a range of performance factors in education, communities and the workplace. In essence, this view sees a positive sense of self leading not just to health and happiness, but to more efficient functioning in all respects.

Perhaps this was best exemplified by the 'California Task Force to Promote Self-esteem and Personal and Social Responsibility' in the 1980s. This initiative, which saw the state legislature investing large sums of money in an attempt to raise the self-esteem of its population, was based on a belief that improving self-esteem would lead to a range of benefits, both for the individual and for society. Not only would schoolchildren and students engage more with their studies, but workers in industry would also become more productive as a result of higher self-esteem. As a consequence, everyone would lead a more fulfilling life and society as a whole would benefit. This view then sees self-esteem as a panacea: a cure for all ills. Those who wish to read more about the California Task Force – including the evaluation of the project – should locate the report referenced at the end of this chapter (California State Department of Education, 1992).

While we are unaware of any similar initiative in the UK, there is little doubt that an industry associated with self-esteem enhancement has grown steadily in recent decades. It is interesting to Google 'self-esteem' and note how many of the hits (and there will probably be over 17 million of them) relate to people or organisations offering help, support or advice – sometimes free, but often at a price. While many of these groups may be well-intentioned, we might hold reservations about some of the others. Certainly, one might be excused for suspecting the motives of some 'conceptual entrepreneurs'. This is a label used by Hewitt (1998) to describe people who see a financial opportunity in convincing others that there is a problem (in this case, low self-esteem) and that they have the solution for it. For teachers with a genuine interest in enhancing the self-esteem of children, the skill is to be able to separate the wheat from the chaff.

If the growth of the self-esteem industry in its widest sense raises some concerns, the picture in education was (initially at least) somewhat less contentious. There were many changes in educational thinking during the 1960s which led to greater interest in the role of self-esteem enhancement in schools. These changes included a move towards the holistic development of children, coupled with a growing awareness of the personal and social needs of individuals. This is a perspective with which many teachers identify, and self-esteem is still seen as a legitimate and important element of the curriculum in primary schools in many countries. This is true both at the level of official policy and individual teacher beliefs. It is certainly a perspective which underpins the work of the current authors. However, having said this, it has to be acknowledged that this is not a universal perspective.

In fact, recent years have seen a 'self-esteem backlash' with teachers, psychologists and philosophers expressing concerns about what they regard as a preoccupation with self-esteem. We shall be looking at some of these concerns later in this book, but one recurring theme is a belief that self-esteem enhancement has achieved prominence at the expense of academic achievement. According to this view, we have been so concerned about protecting children's self-esteem that the quality of learning has suffered; we have 'taken our eye off the ball'. Whether this is true or not, this one issue, perhaps more than any other, has resulted in a polarisation of views on the topic amongst many in education, and indeed in society in general. In the course of this book, we hope to explain why this apparent choice – between enhancing self-esteem or improving learning – reflects a false dichotomy. But that is for later; first we will consider some key ideas from theory and research in the area.

Some important ideas from the literature on self-esteem

As Nicholas Emler pointed out, 'Few ideas in the human sciences have ever achieved the level of attention that has been lavished upon the notion of self-esteem' (2001, p. 2). Certainly, the literature on this topic is vast and is located in many academic disciplines; these include (but are not limited to) philosophy, sociology and psychology. In order to do justice to them all, we would require several volumes – not just a few short chapters! We have therefore had to be very selective and have focused mainly on the psychological literature. Even within this discipline, there are distinctive contributions from different branches of psychology: from cognitive, humanistic, psychoanalytical and social psychology.

Self-esteem research can be traced back over a hundred years to the pioneering writing of William James (1890/1983). For James, our self-esteem reflects the relationship between our successes and our aspirations. In simple terms, feelings of self-esteem are determined by how successful we are in being what we hope to be. If I aspire to be a successful musician and I am making good progress towards that goal, my self-esteem is higher than it would be if I was failing to progress in my musical career. This emphasises an important point which will recur throughout this book – self-esteem is influenced by beliefs about competence.

Another early writer whose ideas remain influential is Charles Horton Cooley. In 1902, he argued that how we feel about ourselves is influenced by what we believe *other people* think of us. This idea – that we take on board the reflected appraisals of significant others – is encapsulated in his idea of the 'looking-glass self'. So, in self-esteem terms, the feedback we receive from other people serves as our looking glass. The point here is that as social animals, we cannot ignore the views that others express, or how others seem to rate us. This idea will also be central to the later chapters of this book.

Since the early writing of James and Cooley (and other influential writers such as George Herbert Mead), work in the area of self-perception has steadily accumulated. We shall be referring to the work of such seminal writers as Stanley Coopersmith, Morris Rosenberg and Carl Rogers, as well as to several more recent contributors. But first there is an important point to be made about the language we employ when we discuss the self.

The language of self-perception

The more one reads about theory and research in the area of self-perception, the more one realises that the terminology is neither consistent nor straightforward. This will become apparent quite quickly.

Let us start with the obvious question. What is self esteem; how has it been defined? Well, in everyday speech at least, we probably share a common understanding of the term. Most would accept that self-esteem is a personal judgement about the self – a judgement which may be either positive or negative. One of the most frequently cited definitions is that of Coopersmith (1967): 'In short, self-esteem is a personal judgement of worthiness that is expressed in the attitudes an individual holds towards himself' (p. 4). Rosenberg, who, alongside Coopersmith, would be considered one of the giants in the field of self-esteem, stated simply that self-esteem is a positive or negative attitude towards the self. More recently,

Roy Baumeister, a prominent writer in this area, said that self-esteem is a favourable global evaluation of the self. The use of the words judgement, attitude and evaluation are central to the issues we raise in later chapters of this book.

While these definitions seem broadly consistent with each other, and with everyday notions of self-esteem, there is a problem. Such definitions would seem to apply equally well to terms such as self-worth, self-regard, self-confidence, self-acceptance and self-respect. Some might argue that they are effectively the same as self-efficacy and self-concept. But, as we shall see in the course of this book, these terms are not synonymous. There are some quite important differences between them and they have been conceptualised and measured in different ways.

(You may want to note down your own definitions of these terms, and compare your list to that which is provided at the end of this chapter.)

Variability in definitions

While most workers in the area would accept the definitions of self-esteem we have provided in the section above, beyond that measure of agreement the picture becomes less clear-cut.

To a certain extent, this variability in terminology reflects the fact that different workers in the field have investigated the self from different perspectives, using different methods and creating different ways of understanding how we value ourselves. For example, even limiting ourselves to the discipline of psychology, self-esteem has been studied from the perspectives of cognitive psychology (Seymour Epstein), behavioural psychology (Stanley Coopersmith), humanistic psychology (Nathaniel Branden), psychodynamic theory (Robert White) and person-centred counselling (Carl Rogers). And this is before we look at writing in the area of philosophy and sociology!

The point is that all of these disciplines have their own frames of reference, methods of enquiry and associated truth criteria. (The last of these refers to what is considered proof or evidence in that discipline.) The consequence is that it becomes difficult to piece together a coherent picture of the field. This lack of agreement can be illustrated by looking at the ways in which writers have linked self-esteem to two other ideas: self-concept and self-worth.

To take the first of these, many writers differentiate self-esteem and self-concept. Self-concept is often considered the highest level of our collection of 'self-words'. From this perspective, self-concept is defined as the sum of the beliefs that individuals hold about themselves. It has both descriptive and evaluative aspects. Descriptive aspects are reflected in self-image, and include gender, occupation, ethnicity, family role, and so on. The evaluative aspects – how we *feel and think* about these characteristics – are reflected in our self-esteem. It can be seen that this definition of self-esteem, emphasising evaluations or feelings about the self, is compatible with the definitions provided above.

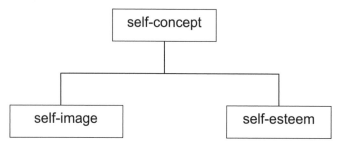

Figure 2.1   The relationship between key self terms

While this perspective is widely accepted, it is not the only view of the relationship between self-concept and self-esteem. For example, Dennis Lawrence, whose publications on self-esteem have provided much helpful advice for teachers over the years, sees self-concept as an umbrella term consisting of three components: self-image, ideal self and self-esteem. This approach has links with earlier work by Carl Rogers, and can be represented by the following diagram:

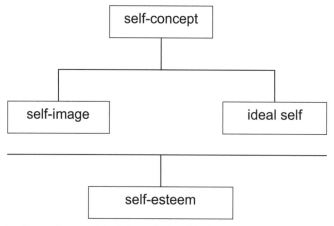

Figure 2.2   An alternative model of the relationship between self terms. Reproduced with permission from Lawrence, 2006, p. 3

According to this model, the self-image is how we currently see ourselves; it is an awareness of our mental and physical characteristics. This seems consistent with its use in the previous diagram. The ideal self is a vision or a model of the person we would like to become. Self-esteem, according to this view, is how we feel about the difference between these two. Stated simply, if our self-image (how we currently see ourselves) is close to our ideal self (what we aspire to be) then our self-esteem is high. We are working towards achieving our goals. Rogers used the term congruence when the actual self or self-image and the ideal self are in harmony in this way. In contrast, if the gap between our self-image and our ideal self is wide, there is a lack of congruence and our self-esteem is correspondingly lower.

Readers may detect similarities with the pioneering work of William James, mentioned earlier. It will be recalled that, for James, self-esteem was the ratio of our successes to our pretensions.

But to return to our discussion about variations in terminology, yet another way of looking at the relationship between self-concept and self-esteem can be found in the writing of one of the leading authorities in the field of self-concept, Herbert Marsh. In his work, overall self-concept is synonymous with self-esteem (see for example, Marsh and Craven, 2006).

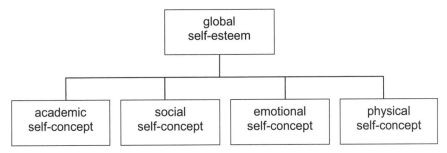

Figure 2.3 A third model of the relationship between self-concept and self-esteem

From this perspective, individuals make judgements about their abilities or performance in different contexts – for example, how successful they are in academic contexts, how competent they feel in social situations, and so on. When taken together, these various judgements combine to create an overall judgement about the self. This overall judgement is called *general self-concept* or *global self-esteem*. Marsh's work is actually more complex than this, and is discussed in more detail below. It will be revisited at several points in the following chapters since it has particular insights to offer teachers.

But to return to the key point about the terminology of self-esteem, even at this early stage in our discussion of self-esteem theory we can see that there are some very basic differences in the way the most fundamental constructs are defined. In fact, there are many other occasions where labels are used in different ways by different authors. For our second example, we mention just one more of these.

A key term in the literature is self-worth. Many writers use this inter-changeably with self-esteem. This is illustrated by the title of Nicholas Emler's useful overview of the research in this area: *Self-esteem: The Costs and Causes of Low Self-worth* (2001), to which we refer later. Self-worth also seems synonymous with the label self-regard, associated with the work of Carl Rogers (1961). However, one particular model, which we discuss at some length in the next chapter, differentiates self-esteem and self-worth. This view, known as a two-dimensional model of self-esteem, sees self-worth as a *component* of self-esteem – with the other component being related to beliefs about competence or efficacy.

Many other inconsistencies are evident in the literature, but enough has been said here to illustrate the point: the field of self-perception is bedevilled by a lack of consensus on terminology. At this point, the enthusiastic but busy teacher might feel a little frustrated by the variety of definitions and beliefs in this area. And, of course, when the picture from academic enquiry is unclear, there is a very real danger that people may fall back on simplistic notions to help explain things.

However, we would encourage readers to be patient a little longer; there are some basic ideas which help us to gain an overview of the field and make sense of it all. In fact, one way to gain a perspective on the wealth of material in the area of self-esteem is to look at the way in which it has been studied in recent years.

Some different approaches to the study of self-esteem

In general terms, there have been three major approaches to the study of self-esteem and these differ in some important respects. The first of these is a *unidimensional* approach, where self-esteem is seen as a generalised feeling of worth. The second approach is really a variant of this, where global self-esteem is seen to be *multi-dimensional* and to comprise different elements. Finally, we have a more complex approach, based on a differentiated, *hierarchical* model, where self-esteem is seen as a set of judgements about performance in different domains. We shall look at each approach in turn, considering the basic principles, the main ways of measuring the phenomenon and the focus of the work that tends to be done from that perspective.

The unidimensional perspective: global self-esteem

When discussing the unidimensional perspective on self-esteem, it is important to acknowledge the contribution of Morris Rosenberg. His work is often regarded as the central reference point in the field. Indeed, his measure of self-esteem (discussed below) is considered the gold standard against which all other self-esteem measures are judged. From this perspective, self-esteem is viewed as a generalised attitude towards the self.

With self-esteem, as with most attitudes, the strength or conviction with which it is held will influence how stable it is. For example, if I have firmly held attitudes in favour of gender equality, these are unlikely to be changed by one or two incidents of a negative nature. Similarly, if I am convinced about my overall self-esteem, it will not be easily changed by short-term setbacks. However, if that attitude is not so firmly held – that is, if I have somewhat mixed feelings about gender equality, or my self-esteem is uncertain – then the attitude is more susceptible to influence from events.

Of course, this is equally true if my attitudes are negative; a firmly held negative attitude towards the self is unlikely to be easily changed by one or two positive but short-term experiences. Unfortunately, many teachers may be able to recall children whose behaviour has illustrated this characteristic. While individuals with high self-esteem are likely to cope with setbacks, and to persevere with difficulties in order to overcome them, those with uncertain self-esteem are more likely to succumb to the challenge and to give up. The implications of such mindsets will be considered in later chapters.

This is not to say that self-esteem never varies; on the contrary, it is accepted that levels of self-esteem can and do vary *somewhat* from day to day. Nevertheless, the point is that we have an overall level of self-esteem which tends to be relatively stable. It may fluctuate a little, but does so around an average level. In this respect, self-esteem can be seen as having the characteristics of both a trait (that is, a relatively consistent personality variable) and a state (in that it can be influenced by the situation one is in). The underlying perspective of the unidimensional model, though, is that in *overall terms* one feels positive or negative about oneself.

This perspective is reflected in measurement terms. Accordingly, the level of overall self-esteem is determined by the sum of the positive statements that individuals make about themselves. If one looks at the Rosenberg Self-Esteem Scale, this becomes clear. Like most self-esteem measures, this is a self-completion scale – in this case, designed originally for adolescents.

---

1. On the whole, I am satisfied with myself.

2. At times I think I am no good at all.

3. I feel that I have a number of good qualities.

4. I am able to do things as well as most other people.

5. I feel I do not have much to be proud of.

6. I certainly feel useless at times.

7. I feel that I'm a person of worth, at least on an equal plane with others.

8. I wish I could have more respect for myself.

9. All in all, I am inclined to feel I am a failure.

10. I take a positive attitude towards myself.

Figure 2.4   The Rosenberg Self-Esteem Scale. Reproduced with permission from Rosenberg, 1965

Respondents indicate whether they agree or disagree with each statement in turn – often using a four- or five-point scale. These ratings are then added up to provide a self-esteem 'score' or 'level'. So we see that such a score or level is simply the sum of the positive statements made about the self. It is also apparent that these are very general in nature; they reflect global evaluations of the self.

Much work in this area has focused on the relationship between global self-esteem and a variety of social and personal problems. For example, low self-esteem has been associated with the incidence of teenage pregnancy and with eating disorders. It is prevalent amongst victims of bullying. It has also been linked with low income and extended unemployment, specifically in males. In terms of psychological health, it has been associated with vulnerability to depression and worse: suicide and suicidal thoughts.

However, as Nicholas Emler (2001) points out in his very useful overview of the evidence, there is a problem in interpreting these apparent links. The evidence available often provides limited information about the *nature* and *direction* of these influences. The point is that self-esteem could be the cause or the consequence of the associated problems. So, we cannot be sure whether low self-esteem contributes to people failing to get a job, or whether it is simply a consequence of being unemployed. Perhaps it is both cause *and* effect. Another possibility is that an *apparent* link – say between teenage pregnancy and low self-esteem – may actually be a result of another factor. For example, multiple partners and a difficulty with relationships might lead to both low self-esteem and unwanted pregnancies. In such a case, the link between low self-esteem and teenage pregnancies is purely incidental.

Of central interest to teachers is the relationship between global self-esteem and educational progress. In fact, many teachers hold a belief that raising self-esteem in children is likely to lead to future educational successes that might not otherwise have been achieved. Unfortunately, the evidence here is not encouraging. There is a relationship between global self-esteem and achievement, but it is not strong. And once more, we have the question about the direction of causality. Does higher self-esteem cause better grades, or do better grades lead to higher self-esteem? Or is something else influencing them both? We examine the issues here in more detail in Chapter 4.

There are other variations on the theme of global self-esteem, including a novel approach which sees self-esteem as a sociometer: a measure of our social acceptance. This idea is associated with the work of Mark Leary (1999) and the argument is that in evolutionary terms, being accepted by the social group has survival value. According to this view, our self-esteem reflects the extent to which we feel we are being accepted by others, and influences our behaviour accordingly. If we feel we are not accepted by others, this is a threat to survival and produces unpleasant feelings typically associated with low self-esteem. We feel the need to gain the approval of others.

A multi-dimensional view of self-esteem

There are several writers in the area of self-esteem who share a focus on the central importance of self-esteem, but who also look at different components of this overall judgement. One of these is Stanley

Coopersmith. Amongst his major contributions to our knowledge of self-esteem has been a recognition of the role that parents play in the development of a child's self-esteem, through their attitudes and their behaviours towards their children. The first version of his Self-Esteem Inventory (Coopersmith, 1967) consisted of 50 items in four sub-scales: peers, parents, school and personal interests. So although this provided an overall or global self-esteem score, it could also be examined to look for information from the four sub-scales.

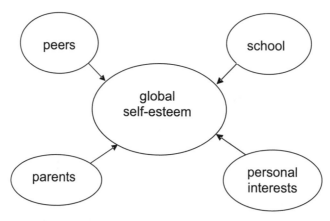

Figure 2.5   Global self-esteem being influenced by different factors

Another example is provided by the work of Susan Harter. In work spanning several decades, she has focused in particular on how children and adolescents develop a view of themselves. In a similar way to Coopersmith, she is interested in overall levels of self-esteem, but also in the nature of self-perceptions in different areas of children's lives. This is reflected in her approach to the measurement of self-esteem. In her 'Self-Perception Profile for Children' (SPPC) (Harter, 1985), a respected and widely-used instrument, she attempts to measure children's perceptions in five areas or *specific domains* – in addition to global self-worth. Harter labels these specific domains as follows: scholastic competence, social acceptance, athletic competence, physical appearance and behavioural conduct. The argument is essentially that an individual's perception of worth in these different domains can vary – but that, in combination, these judgements influence the overall level of self-esteem.

Here are some items from just one of the sub-scales of Harter's SPPC, relating to social competence. It will be noted that these are presented in the form of binary choices; children have to say which statement is most like them.

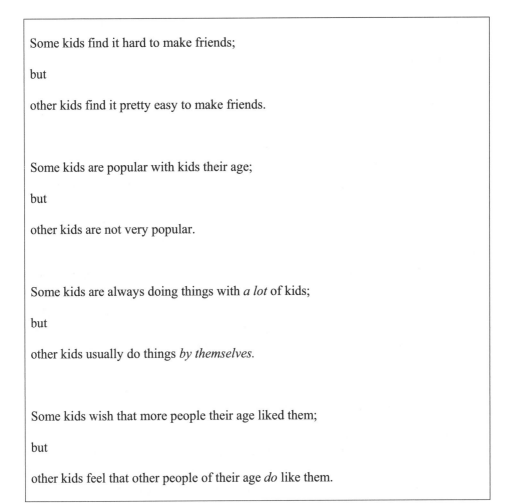

Some kids find it hard to make friends;

but

other kids find it pretty easy to make friends.

Some kids are popular with kids their age;

but

other kids are not very popular.

Some kids are always doing things with *a lot* of kids;

but

other kids usually do things *by themselves.*

Some kids wish that more people their age liked them;

but

other kids feel that other people of their age *do* like them.

Figure 2.6 Items from the social acceptance sub-scale of Harter's SPPC. Reproduced with permission from Harter, 1985

As well as tapping into children's beliefs about their competence in these domains, Harter is also interested in how children *value* these skills or abilities. This relates to a widely held belief in self-esteem circles, going back to the pioneering work of James at the beginning of the 20th century, known as the importance effect. The argument here is that if we value a skill or ability, success or failure will affect our self-esteem; if we don't value it, it is less likely to do so. The importance effect relates to what we call the *contingencies* of self-esteem. A contingency of self-esteem is defined as 'a domain or category of outcomes on which a person has staked his or her self-esteem' (Crocker and Wolfe, 2001, p. 594). So, for a boy who really values football, being dropped from the team is likely to have a negative effect because he stakes his self-esteem on being a good footballer. In contrast, being dropped is unlikely to have a significant effect on the self-esteem of a child who is indifferent towards football; his self-esteem is not contingent upon success as a footballer.

We shall discuss this in more detail in later chapters since these ideas raise many important issues for teachers about the sort of things children base their self-esteem on. The more we know about these contingencies, the better we can help children who experience low self-esteem. Another reason this knowledge is important is because of the links between self-esteem and behaviour, a perennial concern for teachers.

But to conclude this section, we feel obliged to make the following point. Although the notion of the importance effect seems intuitively correct and is implicitly or explicitly supported by many writers in the field, recently it has been called into question. (A reference is supplied at the end of this chapter if you wish to follow this up.) However, we move on now to look at a third and rather different approach to how self-esteem is conceptualised and measured.

The hierarchical model

There are many differences between the hierarchical model and those which emphasise global judgements of self-esteem – even those such as Harter's work, outlined above, which include a multi-dimensional element. These concern the structure of the model (its fundamental nature and how it 'works'), how it is measured and what the information collected is typically used for.

The model can be traced back to the work of Herbert Marsh and Richard Shavelson (see, for example, Shavelson et al., 1976) in the late 1970s and early 1980s. It is most closely associated now with the continuing work of Marsh, currently one of the most prolific writers in the area of self-perception. Strictly speaking, this work is in the area of self-concept rather than self-esteem, but even a brief association with Marsh's writing confirms that he links self-concept and self-esteem very closely[2]. In the self-esteem literature, the model has been employed by O'Brien and Epstein (1983).

In essence, the hierarchical model rests on the belief that how we feel about ourselves is influenced by a series of judgements we make in a variety of different domains. The simplest way of explaining the model is by use of a diagram.

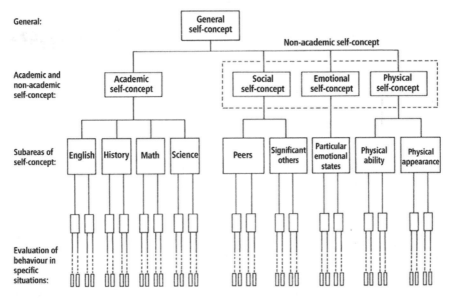

Figure 2.7 The structure of the self-concept. Reprinted with permission from Shavelson et al., 1976, p. 413

A preliminary point here is that this model of the self-concept is based on student populations. A model of self-concept for individuals not in education might contain some changes to these categories, but the essential structure and working of the model would remain. How does it work?

It can be seen from the diagram that general self-concept (or global self-esteem) sits at the top of the hierarchy. Global self-esteem is therefore a cumulative evaluation based on a variety of judgements we make about ourselves – about academic, social, emotional and physical aspects of life. In turn, each of these academic and non-academic aspects of global self-esteem is informed by judgements of competence in several different contexts (sub-areas) which come under that umbrella. So, for example, our global self-esteem is influenced partly by judgements about our social self-concept which in turn is influenced by interactions with peers and with significant others. These sub-areas can themselves be further sub-divided into more specific components which are informed by evaluations in situations where we perform in some way.

Let us take the example of spoken language ability to further explain the working of this model. Starting at the top of Figure 2.7 and working down, we see that our global self-esteem is influenced to a significant extent by academic self-concept; in turn, academic self-concept is influenced by judgements made in the English sub-area. Following the diagram downwards, we see that the English self-concept is influenced by judgements below it – let us say, in talking and listening, reading and writing. If we focus on the talking element, the specific situations in which this might occur could include general class discussions, formal presentations to peers, and so on. Evaluations of performance in this respect will be important not just to judgements in that immediate context, but to all the levels of the hierarchy above.

Several important points follow on from this model. First, the fact that many different evaluations contribute to overall self-esteem helps to explain how our judgements of competence can vary from context to context, while at the same time our overall self-esteem can remain relatively stable.

Second, the model makes clear that the higher levels of the hierarchy – the more generalised evaluations – are being influenced by a variety of messages from specific interactions at lower levels. As the example of spoken language above hopefully illustrates, if we want to enhance self-esteem, we need to look towards the lower levels of the hierarchy for our interventions. The point is that attempts to boost someone's self-esteem by telling them they are doing fine (at a global level) are likely to be ineffective when their more specific judgements – based on first-hand experiences – tell them something altogether different.

Third, it is worth reflecting on the fact that there are two ways of improving our overall self-esteem. One way is to work on the sub-areas, and in particular the specific situations which feed into them: simply stated, to improve our performance. This relates to the point above and will be central to much of the advice in the later chapters of this book. But there is another way.

An alternative method of reducing the negative feelings associated with poor performance is to avoid situations where we feel inadequate. In fact, as adults, we often take this option. If my social self-concept is being negatively affected by the people I meet – for example, in a particular social circle – I will be inclined to spend less time with these people. If my physical self-concept is negatively influenced by my failure to learn basic skills on the tennis court, the chances are that sooner or later I will stop playing; after all, no one likes to feel inadequate. So, we can protect self-esteem by avoiding situations where we feel we are failing – and, as adults with an element of choice, we often do! But, for children, the scope here is more limited. Their world may involve compulsory participation in most or all of the contexts that adults and their peers have set up for them – even when their self-judgements in these contexts are consistently negative. This realisation opens up a range of issues for schools about participation or non-participation, acceptance or refusal, compliance or defiance. We return to such matters later.

What are the issues surrounding measurement of self-esteem when viewed from this hierarchical perspective? When we looked at measurement of global self-esteem, it was seen that the items in the self-report form were very general in nature. In contrast, the items in the measures here tend to be very specific to the domain being investigated.

A measure commonly used for children of primary-school age is the Self Description Questionnaire 1 (SDQ1) (Marsh, 1992). It contains 76 items designed to tap into eight different factors, or aspects of self-concept: Physical Abilities, Physical Appearance, Reading, Mathematics, Peer Relations, Parent Relations, General-Self and General-School. Here is a sample of the items from the SDQ1. (As with many self-report measures, the reader indicates agreement or disagreement on a five-point scale.)

I am good looking

I am good at all **SCHOOL SUBJECTS**

I can run fast

I get good marks in **READING**

My parents understand me

I hate **MATHEMATICS**

I have lots of friends

I like the way I look

Figure 2.8 Items extracted from the Self Description Questionnaire (SDQ1). Reproduced with permission from Marsh, 1992

It can be seen that these items specifically attempt to gauge how the individual feels about him- or herself in different domains or contexts. This reflects both the multi-dimensional nature of self-esteem and also the hierarchical relationships involved. For example, how the respondents feel about their abilities in mathematics and reading should (logically) impact on how they rate their performance on all school subjects; and how they feel about all of these domains will contribute to overall feelings of esteem.

There are many very practical implications for teachers here which will be addressed in the later chapters of this book. These relate to the range of experiences available to children and the messages they receive about their worth and competence. In addition, several very interesting and encouraging messages have emerged from workers in this field. Typically, investigations based on this model have related scores in specific aspects of self-concept to measured performance in corresponding domains. For example, mathematics self-concept has been matched to performance in maths tasks. Such work, often with huge data sets, has highlighted many important processes at work, shedding new light on the relationship between self-concept and school performance. Unlike the messages that emerge from the literature on global self-esteem, these messages are very encouraging in relation to self-esteem and learning. They will be discussed in Chapter 4 when we look at the evidence in relation to education.

Meanwhile, for the final section in this chapter, we move on to think a little about causal processes. What are the experiences which influence how we feel about ourselves? What are the determinants of self-esteem?

What factors influence how you feel about yourself?

At one level, we can probably create a long list of experiences, perceptions and messages which influence how we feel about ourselves as individuals. Obvious esteem-enhancing experiences include success in attaining goals, receiving acclaim from others and feeling one is valued. For children, we assume that experiences such as receiving praise, winning prizes or gaining approval from parents and teachers are likely to enhance feelings of worth. For adults, perceptions that one is doing well in one's career or one's personal life would seem to be obvious causes of enhanced feelings of worth. Beliefs that we are attractive, popular or respected will tend to make us feel better about ourselves. It would be possible for each of us to draw up a long list, although one suspects that many of the items on that list might be personal to the individual concerned.

It is interesting here to note that different writers in the field tend to focus on very different 'causes' of self-esteem. As we discuss at various points throughout this book, many writers (implicitly or explicitly) seem to operate within a rather narrow perspective on how self-esteem is influenced. Even amongst the more 'academic' writers, there are many differences. For example, Emler (2001) maintains that the single largest source of self-esteem is genetics, followed by parental upbringing. Mruk (1999) identifies a wider range of factors which influence self-esteem, and although there is overlap between his list and that of Emler, there are also differences – for example, in relation to birth order, a range of social factors and values. Interestingly, both writers identify experience of success as a factor, and Emler makes the interesting point that our experiences of success influence self-esteem – but not as much as our *perceptions* of those successes. Several of the issues here are revisited later in this book, since they have relevance to what we as teachers can do to enhance self-esteem.

In the meantime, a question arises about whether it is possible – or realistic – to try to identify the processes which influence an individual's self-esteem. Some might argue that the factors that bring high self-esteem are only too obvious – success, wealth, beauty and popularity. The more we have of these things, the higher our self-esteem. However, while this might seem almost 'common sense', the work of Michael Argyle (1969) provides a different perspective on how we form judgements of ourselves. He identifies four major determinants.

First, he argues that our self-perceptions are influenced in the course of social interaction – by the messages we receive from others. To be more accurate (following the early work of Cooley [1902]), our perceptions are influenced by what we *believe* others think of us. Although in this chapter we have pointed out many differences of opinion in relation to self-esteem, this belief – that our self esteem is affected by the messages we get from others around us – is widely accepted. From such messages, we develop a belief that we are worthy, likeable people – or not. We get a feeling that we are accepted into the social group – or not. People appear to respect us and our views – or they do not. It is important to note that these messages can relate to our achievements (our performance or competence in certain domains) or to ourselves as individual humans (irrespective of how talented or successful we are).

The results of this process are most evident with young children. A child who is told she is pretty, helpful, kind and clever is likely to grow up believing it; her self-esteem will reflect such positive messages. In contrast, a child who receives messages from others that she is selfish, or not to be trusted, or useless, is likely to see herself in that way; her self-esteem will reflect this. Even as adults we are not immune from such influences. Many of us have been surprised by a message from someone indicating we are actually doing a bit better than we had previously thought – and have benefited a little in terms of self-belief. Similarly, we may have felt a dip in esteem upon learning that others did not share our own high impression of some achievement or other characteristic. Such self-esteem moments (to use a term associated with the work of Seymour Epstein [1979]) are often related to the messages we pick up from others. We shall return to this idea later.

Second, self-esteem is influenced by comparisons with others, a belief which can be linked to important work by Leon Festinger (1954) in the mid-1950s. The point here is that there seems to be a basic human tendency for us to make comparisons with others in many areas of life. A moment's reflection will probably testify to the validity of that belief – and it is not just when we are striving for some prize or 'sizing up' a rival for a job that we go through this process. Certainly, in such cases it seems a natural process: healthy competition and the survival instinct. But in a less confrontational way, social comparison is characteristic of many day-to-day interactions. It helps us to categorise information and make sense of our world. For example, when you meet new people in a social situation, what is going through your head as you try to decide what 'sort of person' they are? What points of reference are you using when they tell you a little about themselves or their family or their jobs? So, social comparison is a natural human tendency; it plays a significant role in how we make sense of our experiences and is a way of locating ourselves in the social world we live in. For young children, social comparison helps them to make sense of their experiences, to learn how they are doing compared to others and about acceptable and valued ways of behaving.

From a self-esteem perspective, the comparisons we make influence how we feel about ourselves, in particular our sense of achievement. The significant question here is, when we make comparisons with others, *which* others are we comparing ourselves to? Well, in order to have an effect on our self-esteem, the comparisons have to be meaningful. We usually compare ourselves with people of a similar or slightly higher standing. So, an enthusiastic and relatively competent social golfer compares himself to a player of similar or slightly greater skill; this influences how he rates himself as a golfer and influences that aspect of his self-concept accordingly. However, the greater the distance between himself and others, the less meaningful any comparison will be. For our enthusiastic golfer, an unfavourable comparison with the winner of a professional tournament would not impact upon self-concept, because the gap is too wide. The comparison is not meaningful.

All other things being equal, we would expect some comparisons to be favourable, some not; some will enhance our self-esteem, some not. This is what children have to come to terms with; it is what life is about. There are many implications for the classroom, not least of which is the fact that comparisons are made in schools on a daily basis. In fact, we might almost say on an hourly basis; and not just in the classroom – in the playground, the dinner hall and outside the school too. Such comparisons are based on a range of academic, personal, social and cultural factors. They may even be based on criteria which are not fully understood by the children themselves. We return to these concerns in later chapters.

Third, our self-perceptions are influenced by the roles we play. This is an obvious point, perhaps; the role situation in which we find ourselves reflects to some extent the influence we have in society. A related idea is that such roles reflect the trust that a community has placed in us. These factors influence our feelings of worth. A famous study conducted by Robert Merton in 1957 illustrates this neatly. He investigated the effect of occupational roles on the self-concept of medical students. He measured the self-concepts of the medics at the start of their course and again four years later. He found that at the later date they were less likely to see themselves as students but instead tended to see themselves more as doctors. As we know, the role of doctor is a respected one which confers a high status on members of the profession and it is no surprise that this change brought about improvements in self-perception. Many reading this book will be able to reflect back to their professional training and consider how their self-perceptions were influenced when their role changed from being a student to a qualified teacher – again, a valued role in society. In terms of children in the classroom, there are many implications for the roles children choose to play – and the roles that they are required to play. This is particularly so at a time when various forms of peer interaction are becoming mainstream practice in primary schools, and issues surrounding the effects of role on self-esteem are considered in later chapters.

Fourth, self-concept is influenced by identification with models. There are two aspects here which are important: the process of modelling and the role of the model as 'ideal self'. We shall look at each in turn.

The process of modelling is associated with the social learning theory of

Albert Bandura (see for example, Bandura, 1977). It is the process by which an individual acquires social behaviour by copying the actions, responses and apparent emotions of others. The influence of role models on self-esteem is of particular importance when we are thinking of the parent as model. We know that children and young people imitate those who are closest and most important to them. If those people have a healthy self-esteem, we would expect children to benefit accordingly.

This work also receives support from Coopersmith (1967) who high-lighted important links between the behaviours and attitudes of parents and the self-esteem of their children. One of his key findings was a positive relationship between the self-esteem of mothers and their children. The explanation is that parents demonstrate the route to self-esteem by the way they live their lives. As Mruk (1999) put it:

> Parents who face life's challenges honestly and openly and who attempt to cope with difficulties instead of avoiding them thereby expose their children to a pro-self-esteem problem-solving strategy very early. Those who avoid dealing with difficulties reveal a very different route for handling the challenges and problems in life. (p. 75)

Both Coopersmith and Mruk are referring to parents in their roles as models, but parents are not the only role models children encounter – particularly as they grow up. Amongst other models are members of their peer group, sporting heroes, media celebrities, and so on. And, of course, it is an acknow-ledged fact that teachers are also role models for children – particularly so at primary school. The behaviours we demonstrate, the values we share and the attitudes we appear to hold will inevitably have an influence on the self-esteem of our pupils. We shall return to this in later chapters.

The second aspect here is when a role model – or possibly an amalgam of models – becomes the 'ideal self'; that is, the person an individual aspires to become. It will be recalled from what was said earlier in this chapter that the discrepancy between the current self-image and the ideal self influences how we feel about ourselves. It is not necessary to revisit the discrepancy model here, but one point is important. The process of judging progress towards the personal goal one has emphasises an element of *self-referencing* which is not immediately apparent in the other three processes discussed. Such judgements are, in essence, of a different nature from the others identified above (even if they are not immune to influence from such factors). This point will be central to advice in later chapters, in particular when we discuss processes of learning in classrooms, such as formative assessment.

To conclude this section, we believe these four processes, as identified by Argyle (1969), provide helpful insights into how our self-esteem is influenced. In essence, they give us an overview of causal factors at work in an area where beliefs and perspectives vary considerably. Importantly, many implications for the classroom stem directly from these four determinants of self-esteem; they will be central to the advice in the later chapters of this book.

〰 Points to consider

- Which of the major research paradigms do you feel provides most insights for us as teachers?
- What do you feel about the hierarchical model?
- It has been suggested that there are four processes which help to determine levels of self-esteem. Can you relate these to your own experiences?

Chapter summary and conclusion

In this chapter, we have attempted to establish a foundation for the later chapters by providing an overview of some important theoretical issues related to self-esteem. We have acknowledged some early writers in the field, and noted that a number of fundamental ideas from early in the last century are still held to be true today. We next discussed the fact that definitions of self-referent terms are not always shared by the writers in this area.

Next, we looked at three main research paradigms in this area – that is, three ways in which self-esteem has been investigated and the principles and assumptions which underpin those approaches. One approach sees self-esteem as a holistic judgement, based on a generalised feeling of worth. A second approach can be thought of as a development of this model; overall self-esteem can be sub-divided into esteem in several different domains. The third model, rather more complex than the others, views self-esteem in terms of a hierarchical structure, based on a series of judgements in different contexts or domains – both academic and non-academic. All three of these models have important messages for us as teachers.

Finally in this chapter, we looked at some major factors believed to influence our self-perceptions.

What would be really helpful, of course, would be a theory which encapsulated the main insights from these different approaches. The good news is that this can be achieved. In the next chapter, we introduce a relatively recent perspective – one which underpins much of the practical advice contained in the later chapters of this book. It is known as a two-dimensional model of self-esteem. This model is associated with the work of Christopher Mruk (1999).

But why, you may well ask, do we plan to introduce another perspective on self-esteem, when there already seems to be a variety of different perspectives? Are we not simply adding to the uncertainty? Our answer is that we focus on this model in the next chapter for several reasons, the most important of which is that it has helped us – and many teachers and student teachers with whom we have worked – to see a way through the wealth of material in this area. It is able to encompass the insights gained from a huge number of research studies. And, perhaps most importantly of all, it provides a clear sense of direction for teachers in primary classrooms.

Table 2.1 Some key self-referent terms

Self-concept	Self-concept seems to have been conceptualised in different ways, but is usually defined as the overall body of beliefs that an individual holds about himself or herself. It is generally accepted that it includes both descriptive and evaluative judgements.
Self-esteem	Again, this has been defined in different ways, but it usually refers to an evaluation or judgement about oneself. It is how you *feel about* the picture you have of yourself.
Self-image	The way you see yourself. As with many of these terms, there are different interpretations, but essentially self-image is descriptive rather than evaluative.
Ideal self	A notion of the person you would like to become: what you aspire to be. Links can be made with the idea of a role model. The gap between your ideal self and your current self-image is often taken as an indication of your level of self-esteem.
Self-worth	This has two meanings, depending on which model of self-esteem you subscribe to. For many writers, self-worth is synonymous with self-esteem. However, it has a more specific meaning for those who are attracted to the idea of a two-dimensional model of self-esteem, to be explained later. For these people, self-worth is one *component* of self-esteem; it is the extent to which you feel you are leading a good life (based on good principles) and deserving of care and respect from others.
Self-competence	If self-worth (above) is one component of self-esteem, as some writers argue, self-competence is the other component. It is a feeling that you can cope with the challenges you face in life. It has much in common with the idea of self-efficacy (below).
Self-efficacy	Confidence in one's ability to achieve a given task. It tends to be specific to a task, or a relatively narrow set of behaviours – for example, computer self-efficacy. A generalised sense of self-efficacy is similar to what is called 'self-competence' (above).
Self-regard	Self-regard is a term associated with the work of Carl Rogers. In use it seems broadly comparable to self-respect, self-esteem or a positive self-image.

Notes

1 See book 4 of the *Nicomachean Ethics*, D. Ross and L. Braun (trans.) Oxford: Oxford University Press.
2 As we noted earlier, in Marsh's work, he equates general self-concept with overall or global self-esteem. We have followed this convention and in our description use the terms interchangeably.

Further reading 📖

1. If you would like to consult some of the original work of seminal writers mentioned in this chapter, see:
* Argyle, M. (1969) *Social Interaction*. London: Methuen.
* Coopersmith, S. (1967) *The Antecedents of Self-esteem*. San Francisco, CA: Freeman.
* James, W. (1890/1983) *The Principles of Psychology*. Cambridge, MA: Harvard University Press.
* Rogers, C. (1961) *On Becoming a Person*. Boston, MA: Houghton Mifflin.
* Rosenberg, M. (1965) *Society and the Adolescent Self-image*. Princeton, NJ: Princeton University Press.
2. For more on the work of Susan Harter, see:
* Harter, S. (1990) Self and identity development. In S. Shirley & G. Elliot (eds) *At the Threshold: The Developing Adolescent*. Cambridge, MA: Harvard University Press.
* Harter, S. (2011) *The Construction of the Self: Developmental and Sociocultural Foundations*, 2nd edn. New York: Guilford Press.
3. For recent overviews of the research evidence on self-esteem, see:
* Baumeister, R.F., Campbell, J.D., Krueger, J.I. & Vohs, K.D. (2003) Does high self-esteem cause better performance, interpersonal success, happiness or healthier lifestyles? *Psychological Science in the Public Interest*, 4 (1), 1–44.
* Emler, N. (2001) *Self-Esteem: The Costs and Causes of Low Self-Worth*. York: Joseph Rowntree Foundation and YPS.
4. To read a report of the California Task Force to raise self-esteem, see:
* California State Department of Education (1992) *Toward a State of Esteem: The Final Report of the California Task Force to Promote Self-esteem and Personal and Social Responsibility*. Available at: www.eric.ed.gov/PDFS/ED321170.pdf
5. To read more about the importance effect, see:
* Crocker, J. & Wolfe, C.T. (2001) Contingencies of self-worth. *Psychological Review*, 108 (3), 593–623.
* Marsh, H.W. (2008) The elusive importance effect: more failure for the Jamesian perspective on the importance of importance in shaping self-esteem. *Journal of Personality*, 76 (5), 1081–122.
6. For more on the idea of self-esteem as a sociometer, see:
* Leary, M.R. (1999) Making sense of self-esteem. *Current Directions in Psychological Science*, 8 (1), 32–5.

3

Towards a Consensus: A Two-Dimensional Model of Self-Esteem

Key ideas in this chapter

We saw in the previous chapter that there are many important insights to be gained from the extensive literature on self-esteem. Indeed, some beliefs which were introduced over 100 years ago are still relevant today. But we also saw that there are differences in the way self-esteem is conceptualised, the terminology employed and the key messages emerging from different ways of investigating experiences. So, in essence, we have a body of literature which is rich in ideas and diverse in its approaches – but which is not necessarily easy to summarise in a straightforward way to guide the practice of teachers. This chapter aims to address this problem by introducing a two-dimensional model of self-esteem. You will learn about:

- the way in which the two-dimensional model of self-esteem was created
- some research evidence in relation to this model
- the key principles of the model and its messages for what it means to have a healthy self-esteem
- how the model works
- some characteristics of pseudo or defensive self-esteem
- why this model may be useful for teachers.

Preliminary activity for Chapter 3

It is the start of a new term, and you are eagerly anticipating meeting your new class. When reading over the pupil records, you note that the previous teacher has commented specifically on two children who suffer from low self-esteem. From various sources, you learn a bit about the history of the two individuals. Read these short paragraphs and then look at the questions which follow.

Peter is significantly behind his peers in number work and language. Assessments have shown no specific learning difficulties, but low self-esteem has been suggested as a factor. Sometimes he appears upset by the fact that he is doing 'easier' work than his peers – but often it is difficult to motivate him to attempt tasks, and he uses a range of avoidance tactics. Because of illness, his first two years at school were severely disrupted and he has failed to make up lost ground. He seems secure in his relationships with peers and has a stable home background.

Mary is in the top group for maths, and her language work is also good. Although she does well academically, she can sometimes become aggressive if there is an element of competition involved. This can spill over into problems with relationships. She has had a hard time in recent years, with a series of distressing events related to her home life, coupled with some bullying by older children. Perhaps these have influenced her self-esteem. Sometimes she can become very anti-social.

Questions:

1. To what extent do you feel that these (admittedly very brief) summaries might suggest self-esteem problems?
2. What would your first course of action be?
3. Assuming you decide that some self-esteem enhancement activity would be a good idea, identify two or three activities which you might try.

You may want to keep your notes from this task for future reference.

Introduction

When faced with a phenomenon which is vast or complex or challenging, it is a natural response to try to identify a small number of the most important ideas in order to render the information manageable. The need to do this is particularly acute when the knowledge is important to us because we wish to make use of it on a regular basis. So it is with self-esteem. The sheer size of the literature in this area, the variety of self-related terms and the associated lack of consensus are problems that have been commented on by various writers. How can we escape what Neil Smelser (1989) has called 'the definitional maze of self esteem'? How can we organise this wealth of information in a way which takes account of the main theories in the area and the research evidence available? Equally importantly, how can we do this in a way which makes 'real-life sense' to busy teachers?

For us as academics and teachers, the key is to be found in what is known as a two-dimensional model of self-esteem. We first came across this work in the writing of Christopher Mruk (1999). Attempts to provide a truly comprehensive review of the literature on self-esteem are few and far between, but this is one of them. Not only does this work achieve the aim of distilling the key elements in the field, but the theoretical model which emerges from this process seems to offer considerable potential for those of us in education. It seems intuitively 'right' – it resonates with classroom life. Importantly, it appears to provide the answers to many of the questions we – and our students and teachers – have been asking.

In essence, this view sees self-esteem as comprising two interrelated components: self-worth and self-competence. This reflects a fundamental belief that how we feel about ourselves is dependent on two types of judgement, linked to two aspects of the 'value' of a person. These are the intrinsic worth of the individual (what we *are*), and the instrumental value (what we *can do*). The former relates largely to aspects of character, the latter to competence.

In terms of self-perception, the first of these depends on seeing ourselves as worthwhile people who are accepted by others and lead a good life: feelings of self-worth. Such feelings are influenced greatly by the messages we pick up from others (you will remember from Chapter 2 that the process of taking on board such messages was one of the four main determinants of self-esteem). If messages from others suggest we are seen by them as honourable, likeable and trustworthy, we are likely to take these on board and feel a sense of worthiness. But, of course, feelings of worth are not entirely influenced by what others think; our own judgements about the 'rightness' of our conduct and values influence our own sense of worth. If we feel we are living according to an accepted moral code and 'doing the right thing', we feel more worthy.

But in relation to the second issue here – instrumental value – our self-esteem is influenced by how effectively we cope with the challenges we face: feelings of self-competence. This idea is very similar to Bandura's work in the area of self-efficacy (see Bandura, 1992). The term self-efficacy refers to having confidence in our ability to achieve a given goal, based on a range of factors including previous experience of similar tasks. In fact, some authors writing from a two-dimensional perspective of self-esteem tend to use the term efficacy instead of self-competence.

At this point, those with a psychological background may question whether efficacy should really be considered part of self-esteem. In the psychological literature, efficacy is often seen as being independent of self-esteem; it is a cognitive rather than an affective phenomenon (to do with feelings). However, a two-dimensional model of self-esteem involves the belief that coping with the challenges one faces in life (or failing to do so) carries with it subjective feelings about the self. Stated simply, experiences of success and failure are not just registered *at a cognitive level* as efficacy. I am not unmoved by success or failure; as a general rule, alongside the recognition of success or failure is a positive or negative feeling. It influences how I feel about myself. From such a perspective, what we call self-competence is more than just the imprint of efficacy; it is both the cognitive recognition of my success or failure *and* how I feel about it.

A phenomenological analysis

It is not necessary to explain Mruk's technique in detail, but it is helpful to have a general understanding of the process he went through. At the risk of slipping into technical jargon, he employed techniques from what is known as *phenomenological psychology*, defined as 'a way of describing both the individual experience and the universal nature of a given human phenomenon as it is lived in real life' (Mruk, 1999, p. 7). He pointed to some of the difficulties in arriving at an agreed structure of self-esteem, including the fact that the topic is studied from various theoretical perspectives, includes a wide variety of acceptable research methods and involves some special measurement difficulties.

Phenomenological analysis starts by collecting empirical information which is then systematically examined. In his case, he collected information from the most important studies in the area of self-esteem over a period of more than a century. He then analysed these in detail, and the end result of this process was the identification of 'the big picture' – that is, the universal components of the phenomenon – and also an understanding of how these are experienced by the individual. So, in this case, we were provided with a model of how self-esteem should be conceptualised (the bigger picture) but also an explanation of what it means to individuals in the reality of day-to-day life.

One key message that emerges from this analysis is that many approaches to the study of self-esteem have been incomplete in their focus. They have tended to fall into one of two camps: those which focus primarily on self-worth, and those which concentrate on judgements of competence. For example, Mruk points out that although the writing of Stanley Coopersmith (1967) does make reference to competence, the main emphasis of his work has been on self-worth, as exemplified in his famous definition of self-esteem as being a personal judgement of worthiness expressed in our attitudes towards ourselves. Certainly, the work of Carl Rogers (1961) is clearly focused on the worth dimension. On the other hand, the seminal work of William James (1890/1983) and the psychodynamic writing of Robert White (1963) more clearly reflect a concern with competence.

Now, the point being made here is not that any of these studies were misguided, or unsound – or the findings unhelpful or questionable. Quite the reverse: they have all added to our understanding of how individuals perceive themselves; they have provided important insights to move our thinking forward. It is simply that such investigations in themselves supply only a partial picture. Mruk's argument is that any complete model of self-esteem must include reference to both component elements: self-worth *and* self-competence.

As a result of his analysis, Mruk developed a two-dimensional model and demonstrated that this is capable of incorporating the findings of the main work published in the area of self-esteem. Since Mruk conceptualises self-esteem as the integrated sum of self-worth and self-competence, this means that for individuals to have high self-esteem they must feel confident *both* about their sense of self-worth ('I am a good person, entitled to care and respect from others') and their sense of self-competence ('I am able to meet the challenges I face in life'). According to this model, if individuals have a deficiency in one or other dimension, they may behave in ways which suggest high self-esteem, but such characteristics may in fact reflect what is called *pseudo* or *defensive* self-esteem. To explain this, it is helpful to refer to the following diagram.

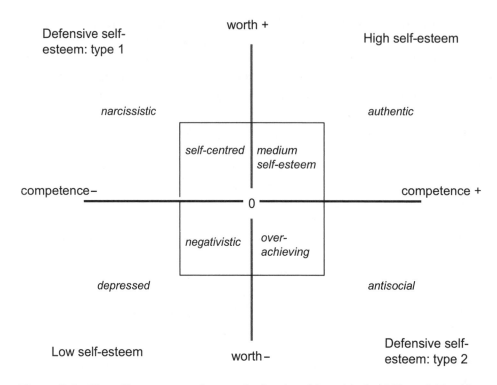

Figure 3.1 The self-esteem meaning matrix. Reprinted from Mruk, 1999, p. 165, with kind permission of Springer Science and Business Media

Mruk's model sees the two dimensions of self-esteem intersecting each other at a central point. Feelings of self-worth are represented in the diagram by the vertical blue line; these vary between positive feelings of worth at the top of the diagram, through a neutral position represented by the zero, to a negative sense of worth at the bottom. Similarly with competence, represented by the horizontal green line, we see a negative sense of competence on the left, and positive on the right. This creates four quadrants to the model, and each of these represents a different self-esteem condition. In turn, each of these conditions is sub-divided into clinical and non-clinical conditions. (The non-clinical conditions are represented within the four smaller squares, where most people are likely to be located. The clinical conditions would be towards the extremes of each quadrant.)

So what can we learn about these conditions? Two of them are consistent with what is widely believed about high self-esteem and low self-esteem. Two of them, at least initially, appear less familiar. Let us start with the familiar ones.

According to the model, individuals who are low both in self-competence and self-worth have classic low self-esteem; they are represented by the lower-left quadrant of the diagram. They are likely to behave in ways that are familiar to many teachers. They tend to be negativistic in outlook; they are reluctant to contribute to new activities, have negative perceptions of their own abilities and low expectations of favourable outcomes. Of course, such perceptions on the part of individuals are often a result of a history of negative outcomes, both in terms of their achievements and the way they have been treated (or mistreated) by others. In clinical conditions, this may result in depression and worse. Such a perspective is completely consistent with the evidence which links low self-esteem with a range of mental health problems, including clinical depression and being a precursor to suicide attempts.

In contrast, if we look at the top-right quadrant of the diagram, we find those who have a positive sense of worth and competence: high self-esteem. Such individuals have a more positive outlook on life, tend to be keen to take on new challenges, have high expectations of success, and so on. Their sense of worth is likely to reflect positive messages received from others about their personality traits, together with a belief that they are conducting their lives according to accepted moral codes. In parallel to this, their feelings of self-competence will be based on a history of competence and achievement in various domains – in all likelihood, demonstrated both to themselves and others.

Such descriptions are familiar to anyone who has an interest in self-esteem; they are almost stereotypes, in fact. But, as would be expected, there is a wide range within the category of positive self-esteem. In fact, this model distinguishes between the majority of individuals in this category, whom Mruk (1999) describes as having medium self-esteem, and a much smaller minority who enjoy particularly high perceptions in both categories, who are described as having *authentic* high self-esteem. Statistically speaking, it is likely that most people with a positive sense of both worth and competence would fall into the category of medium self-esteem.

An interesting aspect of this model is the identification of two other categories of self-esteem; these are the two quadrants (top-left and bottom-right) which are labelled defensive self-esteem. It would be a mistake (though possibly a common one) to interpret these two conditions as being the same, effectively representing people who just have less in the way of overall self-esteem. To adopt this view would be to ignore the key message: a person may have a positive sense of self-worth but not necessarily of self-competence – and vice versa. A deficiency in one dimension is not the same as a deficiency in the other. They are based on different sets of appraisals and are associated with different patterns of behaviour. So, what do these look like?

When we refer to the idea of defensive self-esteem (sometimes known as pseudo-self-esteem), we are describing individuals who act as though they have high self-esteem when in fact they have a serious deficiency in one of the two components. The model illustrates this phenomenon by identifying what are called defensive type 1 and defensive type 2 conditions. As we can see from the model, defensive type 1 individuals have a positive sense of worth but not of competence. In a classroom, such children may appear quite confident but have learned that they are often not able to perform age-appropriate tasks effectively. A consequence of this is that when the demonstration of some kind of competence is called for, they may feel threatened and employ various avoidance and/or denial strategies. They may also appear boastful and over-confident. We shall look at such characteristics in more detail in a later chapter, since they are central to any attempts to enhance self-esteem.

In contrast, individuals who would be categorised as defensive type 2 are faced with a different set of self-appraisals and tend to display different behaviour characteristics. In Figure 3.1, these people can be seen in the bottom-right quadrant. They are positive in terms of self-competence but low in self-worth. A typical scenario here is a person with a secure sense of competence based on experiences of success, but with a low sense of worth because of distressing or traumatic events, a history of negative messages from others about their worth, or doubts about the way they are conducting their own lives. Such people may attempt to compensate for the negative feelings associated with a low sense of worth by focusing – sometimes obsessively – on demonstrating their competence. While such behaviour may have some benefits (not least in terms of productivity), their behaviour patterns are likely to include a range of anti-social behaviours. The difference between the two defensive self-esteem conditions is central to the advice which follows in the later chapters of this book.

A brief interlude

At this point, having read this brief outline of the two-dimensional model, it might be interesting to reflect on the characteristics associated with the four conditions and try to find an example of each type of individual. You may want to think about children in a class – or adults you have met. In particular, you may find it interesting to look for examples of individuals who display characteristics of defensive self-esteem.

Further support for a two-dimensional model of self-esteem

Mruk's (1999) analysis is certainly the most comprehensive explanation of the two-dimensional model of self-esteem, but further theoretical support for this perspective can be found in the writing of the humanistic psychologist Nathaniel Branden (1969, 1994). In fact, Mruk acknowledges this in his own work, and for those who find Mruk's texts somewhat challenging, Branden's books provide a very readable discussion of self-esteem from a two-dimensional perspective.

But there are also other sources of support for this approach to the study of self-esteem. Romin Tafarodi and various associates (for example, Tafarodi and Milne, 2002; Tafarodi and Swann, 1995) have provided empirical support; that is, they have gathered experimental evidence which supports the two-dimensional nature (the *duality*) of self-esteem. It is likely that most readers will be less interested in the technicalities of these studies than in the messages that emerge from them. However, two particular studies are briefly outlined since they provide empirical support for the two-dimensional model of self-esteem; that is, they provide 'hard' research evidence to support the theoretical ideas.

The first of these studies established that a two-dimensional model of self-esteem can explain the pattern of self-esteem scores in a group of people. The second study looked at how events which influence feelings of worth or competence affect people's self-esteem scores. It demonstrated that the two dimensions – competence and worth – were indeed independent of each other.

From Chapter 2 it will be recalled that Morris Rosenberg's (1965) work reflected a global view of self-esteem; that is, self-esteem is a positive or negative attitude towards the self. Rosenberg's Self-Esteem Scale (known as the RSES), which we looked at briefly in the last chapter, is considered by many to be the 'gold standard' in self-esteem research. Importantly, it had been considered unidimensional in nature. However, in a series of experiments, Tafarodi and his colleagues asked over a thousand students to complete the RSES; they then analysed the results to see whether the patterns of responses pointed to a unidimensional or a two-dimensional structure for self-esteem.

The findings pointed to the latter explanation; they concluded that self-esteem was not just one-dimensional but consisted of two factors which they called self-competence and self-liking. Although their terminology is not identical to that which we use above, the similarity in terms of the underlying principle is clear. On one hand, we see the more objective, performance-based judgements which contribute to feelings of self-competence; on the other, there are the subjective feelings of worthiness – what we might call internalised positive regard from others. The researchers concluded that a model based on these two factors better explained the nature of self-esteem than the unidimensional model which had always been associated with Rosenberg's work.

Another experiment provided further evidence that self-worth and self-competence are different aspects of self-esteem. The researchers did this by matching up changes in scores in self-worth and self-competence with intervening life events. It was found that students who suffered negative events related to achievement, such as failure or frustration, had lowered scores in terms of self-competence. In contrast, negative messages from others, such as rejection or disapproval, tended to reduce scores for worth. An additional extra finding from these studies was that people who were already low in one aspect of self-esteem tended to be particularly sensitive to negative messages in that area. So, students whose scores had indicated low self-competence were quickest to recognise words which reflected a deficit in competence. In contrast, those students low in self-worth were quicker to recognise words which suggested a deficit in that area. There are implications here for teachers which we shall return to in later chapters.

There is a lot more to be said about the theoretical and empirical basis of the two-dimensional model of self-esteem, but we feel enough has been said here to establish the validity of the approach. In particular, the three main sources of support for the two-dimensional approach seem to complement each other. The writing of Nathaniel Branden, particularly in his book *The Six Pillars of Self-esteem* (1994), was based on case studies and philosophical argument, and provided a clear account of the two-dimensional model. Later on, Christopher Mruk (1999) used different techniques, from phenomenological psychology, to look at the theoretical and empirical evidence in order to construct his model. Over a similar period, but independently of both Branden and Mruk, Romin Tafarodi and various colleagues were using traditional experimental techniques, showing that a two-dimensional model was better able to explain the patterns of self-esteem scores than alternative models. It is significant that these different approaches all provide a consistent message about the value of the two-dimensional model.

If further indication of the value of this model were needed, in recent years two dimensional measures of self-esteem have been used in several published studies, in higher education, primary education and other areas such as health-related research. Those related to primary education will be discussed in the next chapter, but further evidence of the growing acceptance of this view of self-esteem is reflected in the official views expressed by the National Association for Self-Esteem (NASE). (The link for this can be found at the end of the chapter.) For us, there is little doubt about its theoretical credentials, and in later chapters you will be able to judge for yourself its practical value – its usefulness in guiding your practice in the classroom.

Implications for teachers

There are many implications for teachers which stem from this work, and in essence they provide the core for this book. Some of them will be discussed in the next chapter where we look at the messages that schools and teachers can take from self-esteem research. Thereafter, they will form the basic structure for the practical strategies we describe. But we would like to end this chapter with two general messages that we feel are worth reflecting upon.

For us, the main advantage of the two-dimensional model is that it provides a clear conceptual framework through which to view self-esteem in the classroom. As we explained in the last chapter (and as will be further illustrated in Chapter 4), although the field of self-esteem is rich in information and insights, it is not easy to assimilate the wealth of material in a way which provides a sense of direction in the classroom. But the two-dimensional model can help us here by providing a relatively straightforward way of informing ongoing practice. It is a lens through which we can view the interactions which are typical of primary classrooms. As a direct consequence, we are able to see more clearly how day-to-day experiences in our own classrooms can influence feelings of worth and competence. You will be able to judge for yourself whether this is so as you read through the later chapters.

But there is another message which emerges from the two-dimensional model; this concerns the prevailing view about self-esteem enhancement techniques in primary classrooms in recent years. There seems little doubt that the emphasis in terms of self-esteem strategies has been on activities to help children feel valued, often encouraging a sense of self-worth by emphasising the unique attributes of each individual child. Children have been encouraged to see themselves as special. Teachers have been advised to see praise as the key enhancement technique. Central to this process is the establishment of a classroom climate in which children are listened to, respected and helped by adults and peers alike. Many readers will recognise the worth-building perspective which underpins most of the activities encouraged in self-esteem books for primary school teachers (see, for example, a selection listed at the end of the chapter).

Now, it is widely accepted that self-worth is important for the happiness and mental health of all individuals. In schools, it is completely consistent with the 'whole-child' perspective which is a cornerstone of much primary practice in the UK and elsewhere. But, obviously, a two-dimensional perspective on self-esteem prompts us to ask whether the self-competence dimension has received as much attention in recent years. The answer to this is not immediately clear, but anecdotal feedback from teachers and students leads us to suspect not. However, if we accept the need to have a balanced approach to self-esteem enhancement, it is *necessary* to complement such self-worth activities with techniques designed to develop a sense of competence or efficacy. Although this may come as little surprise to many reflective teachers who have gained insights into the perceptions of their pupils, for many it may require a slight re-examination of beliefs and practices.

At this point, the sceptical reader, or the teacher who is happy with current practice in relation to self-esteem, might argue that the criticism offered here in relation to current classroom practice is unjustified. They might claim that there are many activities, exemplified in current texts and curriculum materials, which focus on emphasising achievement as a source of self-esteem. For example, children are often encouraged to identify their talents and tell others what they are 'good at'. But there is a fundamental point to be made here. While there may be a place for 'finding' achievements of which we are proud, and indeed telling others about these, it should not be confused with the *process of creating* a genuine sense of competence based on new achievement.

As Mruk (1999) points out, a sense of competence, unlike a sense of worth, tends to be based in large measure on observable behaviours – that is, performance of some sort. In order to increase a sense of competence, it is not helpful to tell children they are good at something when it is evident, both to them and to others, that they are not. Instead, it is necessary to provide the opportunity for them to achieve real success – and then to help them recognise it as such. A distinction has to be drawn between these two perspectives on encouraging a sense of competence. It is essentially the distinction between a generalised 'feel-good' climate and an alternative approach which focuses on techniques specifically designed to *create* new achievement – and so develop self-competence.

Obviously, this begs the question, if current self-esteem enhancement approaches provide at best a partial answer, what should teachers do? We argue that the development of self-competence is unlikely to be achieved by selecting superficially appealing activities from current commercial resources; it is more likely to be encouraged by reconsidering some fundamental aspects of day-to-day teaching and learning. Following the next chapter, which looks at what we can take from research evidence in schools, we begin that process.

〰️ Points to consider

Revisit the preliminary activity you undertook at the start of this chapter. In the light of what you have now read, consider the following questions:

1. What would you now want to learn more about in order to help these two children?
2. To what extent do you think the two dimensions of self-worth and self-competence might help to explain the condition of these children?
3. To what extent do you think the two dimensions give a sense of direction about the best course of action for you as a concerned teacher?
4. Revisit your suggestions for ways of helping the two children. How might you now begin to formulate a plan?

You may want to keep your notes from the third question to refer to when you read the later chapters.

Chapter summary and conclusion

The two-dimensional model of self-esteem emerged from a comprehensive phenomenological analysis of work in the area of self-esteem. A key principle that underpins the approach is that any complete model of self-esteem must encompass *both* feelings of worth and judgements of competence. It leads to the definition of self-esteem as the integrated sum of these two components. Its importance to individuals is encapsulated in Nathaniel Branden's words: 'It is the conviction that one is competent to cope and worthy of living' (1969, p. 110). If an individual has a negative sense of worth or competence, he or she would be described as having pseudo or defensive self-esteem. There are typical behaviours which may be associated with individuals in such situations. A two-dimensional model of self-esteem also has support from empirical research studies conducted with university students, other adults and school pupils. This model may be useful for teachers for several reasons, in helping them to understand how self-esteem works and by providing them with a conceptual model to guide their practice.

The next chapter, which looks at self-esteem specifically in relation to school, focuses on the messages teachers can take from self-esteem research. Amongst the studies reported are some using a two-dimensional model to investigate children's learning in primary classrooms.

Further reading 📖

1. If you wish to read in more detail the key writings of Christopher Mruk, see:
- Mruk, C. (1999) *Self-esteem: Research, Theory and Practice*. London: Free Association Books.
2. As indicated in this chapter, Mruk acknowledges the influence of Nathaniel Branden. His writing is very accessible and provides a good introduction to the two-dimensional model of self-esteem:
- Branden, N. (1969) *The Psychology of Self-esteem*. New York: Bantam Books.
- Branden, N. (1994) *The Six Pillars of Self-esteem*. New York: Bantam Books.
3. To read about some of the empirical studies conducted by Romin Tafarodi and his colleagues, see:
- Tafarodi, R.W. & Milne, A.B. (2002) Decomposing global self-esteem. *Journal of Personality*, 70 (4), 443–83.
- Tafarodi, R.W. & Swann, W.B. Jr. (1995) Self-liking and self-competence as dimensions of global self-esteem: initial validation of a measure. *Journal of Personality Assessment*, 65, 322–42.
4. To learn more about the National Association for Self-Esteem (NASE), see:
- the home page at www.self-esteem-nase.org/index.php
- a short piece on that website by Robert Reasoner on *The true meaning of self-esteem*, which illustrates how that organisation has adopted a two-dimensional model of self-esteem (www.self-esteem-nase.org/what.php).

5. For other research studies which use the two-dimensional model of self-esteem to investigate a range of health issues, see, for example:

- Sassaroli, S. & Ruggiero, G.M. (2005) The role of stress in the association between low self-esteem, perfectionism, and worry, and eating disorders. *International Journal of Eating Disorders*, 37, 135–41.
- Surgenor, L.J., Maguire, S., Russell, J. & Touyz, S. (2006) Self-liking and self-competence: relationship to symptoms of anorexia nervosa. *European Eating Disorders Review*, 15 (2), 139–45.

6. Some popular books written for primary teachers on self-esteem enhancement, illustrating the predominantly self-worth perspective, are:

- Canfield, J. & Wells, H.C. (1994) *100 Ways to Enhance Self-Concept in the Primary Classroom*. Boston, MA: Allyn & Bacon.
- Curry, M. & Bromfield, C. (1994) *Personal and Social Education for Primary Schools through Circle Time*. Tamworth: NASEN.
- Mosley, J. (1993) *Turn Your School Round*. Cambridge: LDA.
- Mosley, J. (1996) *Quality Circle Time in the Primary Classroom*. Cambridge: LDA.
- Wetton, N. & Cansell, P. (1993) *Feeling Good: Raising Self-Esteem in the Primary School Classroom*. London: Forbes.

4

Self-Esteem and Schools

Key ideas in this chapter

In earlier chapters, we noted the existence of debates and uncertainties surrounding self-esteem. Nowhere are these issues more keenly debated than in the world of education.

In this chapter, you will learn about:

- current and recent debates in relation to self-esteem in school, including the criticisms from the 'anti-self-esteem lobby'
- the messages for education from research evidence in self-esteem
- insights from classroom studies using a two-dimensional model
- some guiding principles for teachers and schools.

Introduction

For many years now, primary school practice, certainly in the UK, has placed great emphasis on the importance of self-esteem. The reasons for this may be two-fold. The first is related to a concern, deeply embedded in primary pedagogy, for the 'whole child'; that is, the social and emotional aspects of development, as well as the cognitive aspects. Such basic principles can be traced back to Rousseau and, for most teachers, are reason enough for schools to help children to develop positive self-perceptions (see Rousseau, 1979). The second reason relates to a belief that gains in self-esteem will lead to improved attainment; in essence, children who feel good about themselves are more likely to fulfil their potential. However, this is hotly contested by those on different sides of the self-esteem fence. While the situation is not as clear-cut as many would hope, the conflicting evidence can be reconciled to provide a clear picture for teachers. But before we look at the evidence, it is worth considering the context in which the debate is situated.

The concerns of the 'anti-self-esteem lobby'

Many writers have commented on the growth of the self-esteem industry, particularly in the 1980s and early 1990s. Certain characteristics have been discussed in earlier chapters, with self-esteem being seen as a 'silver bullet' to cure a range of educational and social ills. As a consequence, school systems in many countries raised the status of self-esteem as an educational goal.

But, as with many social phenomena, a counter-movement developed; this has since been labelled the 'anti-self-esteem lobby' or the 'self-esteem backlash'. It came to prominence in the early 1990s, with many writers being critical of what they saw as an obsession with self-esteem. There are several strands to the criticism and, while there is not scope here to look at all of them, one is of particular concern to teachers. It is the assertion that the promotion of self-esteem as an educational goal has been damaging for education.

This criticism is often directly related to practices which followed on from beliefs about 'protecting' self-esteem in the classroom. Some of these techniques were described earlier and include schools developing a culture of constant praise, avoiding experiences of failure, playing down competition, making each child feel unique, and so on. Central to this was the role of the teacher in relentlessly 'building up' children's opinions of themselves, in the belief that this would help them succeed – not just in school, but in life generally. The approach is exemplified in this description of a self-esteem-enhancing school:

> [E]ach classroom I visited was dedicated to the mission of pumping up every student's confidence. One teacher exclaimed, 'You can do anything, can't you?'; another wore a button with a diagonal red slash running through the words 'I can't'. Bulletin boards featured such slogans as 'You are beautiful!' And classes were required [...] to recite 'I am somebody' each morning. (Kohn, 1994: 276)

We suspect that many readers will share our reservations about the value of some of these practices. It is possible that they were driven by mistaken beliefs about the nature of self-esteem and how it can be influenced, coupled with a naïve perspective on the consequences in classrooms. But whatever the reasons, such questionable practices provided plenty of ammunition for those who wanted (for a variety of reasons) to criticise self-esteem as an educational goal. In a way, they provided an easy target. We now look at some of these critiques, highlighting the main arguments and offering some of our own thoughts on these issues.

In the academic literature, an early critical perspective was that of William Damon (1995) who claimed that the emphasis on self-esteem was not leading to mature or competent individuals; indeed he argued that it had resulted in falling standards in competence and behaviour. His view was that self-esteem 'offers nothing more than a mirage' to parents and teachers, resulting in us ignoring more important aspects of children's development, such as learning good work habits and the social and moral aspects of character formation. Although his observations were set in a particular historical and cultural context (mid-1990s America), many writers express similar concerns today (see, for example, Twenge and Campbell, 2009).

Around the same time, Martin Seligman, now a leading authority in the field of positive psychology, raised similar issues (1995). He argued that an over-emphasis on how a child feels about himself or herself – at the expense of what he or she actually *does* – may in fact be counter-productive in terms of confidence and personal growth. Indeed, it seems obvious that children who never face challenges (because of policies to avoid failure at all costs) and who never have to strive to overcome setbacks, are unlikely to develop any kind of self-reliance or resilience.

While these authors highlight very real problems, it is important to note the way in which the debate is framed; self-esteem is placed *in opposition to* other important aspects of development and performance. Consequently, schools choose to enhance self-esteem *or* they focus on these other important skills. We do not subscribe to this view. As we illustrate in subsequent chapters, a realistic and informed perspective on self-esteem is set within frameworks which include moral issues and social learning in the classroom. A realistic sense of self-esteem is also intimately related to high expectations and improving performance. In short, self-esteem enhancement is not promoted *at the expense of* these important aspects of development; it is intimately bound up with them.

To return to the critique of self-esteem: more recently, Richard Smith (2002) has questioned the wisdom of over-valuing self-esteem as an educational goal, not least for the inward-looking perspective which it can encourage. He asked whether education should encourage children to be looking outwards towards others, rather than in on themselves. This seems a legitimate point, certainly if teachers devote a disproportionate amount of time each day to techniques which encourage introspection. Our argument would be that they need not; indeed, they should not.

Many criticisms of previous practices concern the techniques employed to 'protect' self-esteem. Ruth Cigman (2001) argued that there is an element of insincerity or disrespect towards children when they receive disproportionate levels of praise because teachers fear damaging their self-esteem. She also pointed to the tensions between, on the one hand, protecting children's self-esteem and, on the other, allowing them to experience failure – particularly when failure can be an important aspect of the learning process. The over-use of praise seems to be a recurring theme with critics, and not without some justification. Elliott (2002) reported that teachers in the UK and USA (unlike several other countries) tended to give over-positive messages to their pupils about their ability – messages that did not accurately reflect the teachers' true assessment of their children's abilities. There are numerous social and cultural factors here, but one important reason is believed to be teachers' reluctance to offer negative comments for fear of damaging self-esteem.

Certainly, the over-use of praise seems ill-advised, and in later chapters we argue for a more nuanced understanding here. There are different types of praise and they serve different purposes, but it may be that many teachers have been operating with a limited understanding of the relationship between praise and self-esteem. We differentiate contingent and affirming praise and highlight the dangers of disproportionate praise and what is called non-contingent success.

Although many of the criticisms above seem reasonable and merit our attention, Kohn (1994) has observed that, in general, the tone of self-esteem commentaries has 'ranged from harshly critical to downright snide'. Some may recognise similar trends today. Certainly, Polly Toynbee (2001) exemplified the passions which seem to surround the issue of self-esteem. Writing for *The Guardian* following the publication of Nicholas Emler's review of the research evidence, she titled her piece, 'At last we can abandon that tosh about low self-esteem'. The sub-title, 'The psychobabblers' snake-oil remedies have been exposed as a sham' gives a further flavour of the approach adopted.

In fact, several writers have commented on the limitations of the argument from both sides in the self-esteem debate and such limitations are also evident amongst the policy makers. Emler (2001) referred to the simplistic understandings which often inform policy initiatives, drawing attention to the influence of 'conceptual entrepreneurs' who see the prospect of financial gain in the public concern with self-esteem. Certainly, many teachers will be only too aware of a range of initiatives (in several areas of the curriculum) which appear to have been driven more by commercial interests – or educational fashion – than by sound understanding of the teaching and learning process.

Even from this necessarily brief overview, it is apparent that there are several different strands to the self-esteem debate. These relate to the purpose of education, the role of self-esteem within this, the methods employed to enhance self-esteem and the evidence related to this. But, despite the number and complexity of these issues, Covington (2001) has pointed out that the debate is often reduced to a question of whether we want children to be good learners or to *feel good* about themselves. We have already noted this as a feature of some of the critical commentaries above.

Such oversimplification is unhelpful, since it actually misrepresents the relationship between self-esteem and learning. Trying to enhance self-esteem and having high expectations of performance and conduct are not alternative priorities – they are not competing demands on a teacher's time. As the previous chapter suggested, there is a close relationship between performance and self-esteem; stated simply, coping with new challenges enhances beliefs about competence. Similarly, there is a close relationship between conduct (in terms of moral and social factors) and feelings of self-esteem; being valued because of the way you live your life influences feelings of self-worth.

What is the evidence about self-esteem and school performance?

For many teachers, a fundamental question is, does improving children's self-esteem lead to better learning? On the face of it, it is hard to say; the messages emerging from the literature seem to contradict each other. In essence, there are two main sets of evidence that we need to consider: that which relates global self-esteem to achievement, and that which relates *more specific* aspects of self-esteem (or self-concept) to achievement. We shall look at each in turn before considering additional information from some recent classroom studies.

Evidence in relation to overall or global self-esteem

Two thorough and well-respected reviews of the research evidence have arrived at the conclusion that the links between global self-esteem and academic performance are not convincing. Roy Baumeister, a respected academic and an authority in this area, investigated the relationship between self-esteem and a variety of favourable outcomes, one of these being school attainment. In the process of gathering together all the relevant evidence, he and his colleagues became aware that:

> Although many thousands of publications refer to self-esteem, relatively few of them report studies that used highly rigorous methods to examine the causal impact of self-esteem on personal and social problems. (Baumeister et al., 2003, p. 10)

Their analysis included only those publications which met strict criteria in terms of quality. They concluded that the modest relationship between self-esteem and attainment did not support the belief that gains in self-esteem lead to better school performance. They were also critical of what was done in the name of self-esteem enhancement in schools, as illustrated by the quote from Kohn given earlier in this chapter.

Very similar findings were reported by Nicholas Emler, whose work we have already mentioned. He was commissioned by the Joseph Rowntree Foundation to conduct a review of the evidence in relation to self-esteem. The results of this endeavour were published in 2001 in his book, *Self-Esteem: the Costs and Causes of Low Self-Worth*. As we pointed out earlier, he also concluded that there was a relationship between self-esteem and school performance, but it was a modest one. Furthermore, because of the nature of the research evidence available, it was not possible to say whether high self-esteem leads to improved performance or the other way round.

Taken together, these influential studies may be disappointing for many self-esteem enthusiasts, for if there is little 'hard' evidence that improvements in self-esteem increase the likelihood of academic success, then one of the principal reasons for devoting time to esteem-enhancement activities is called into question. But is the picture as uncertain as this? Well, there exists another body of evidence which we need to consider.

More specific aspects of self-esteem: academic self-concept

It will be recalled from Chapter 2 that there have been different ways of conceptualising self-esteem. One of these is the unidimensional or global model; another is the hierarchical model, often associated with the work of Herb Marsh and his associates (see for example, Marsh and Shavelson (1985); Marsh and Craven (2006). You may wish to remind yourself of the main features of this model (see page 27). In particular, remind yourself how global self-esteem, sitting at the top of the hierarchy, is influenced by more specific aspects of self-esteem (or self-concept) at lower levels. (Note also that we follow Marsh's convention of using 'self-concept' when discussing specific aspects of self-esteem.)

The extensive investigations of Marsh and his associates involved sophisticated statistical techniques with huge data sets, and this work has led them to very different conclusions from the reviews we have just looked at. Instead of looking at how *overall* or *global self-esteem* relates to performance, they focused on those *specific aspects* of self-esteem which seem most closely related to the task in hand. For example, they focused on beliefs about competence in maths (what they call *mathematics self-concept*) and related these to performance on specific maths tasks. Their findings paint a different picture from work which focuses on global self-esteem.

Stated simply, when we look at *specific aspects* of self-esteem, there is an effect on performance *over and above* that of ability alone. So, improved self-concept in a given domain (essentially, beliefs about competence in that domain) can indeed contribute to improved performance. The relationship between these specific aspects of self-belief and the associated tasks is formalised in their *reciprocal effects model* (REM). Interested readers can learn more about this work in Marsh and Craven (2006).

So we see a plausible explanation for the fact that previous work had shown no clear relationship between self-esteem and performance. It is that such work was based on global measures of self-esteem – and, as we have seen from earlier chapters, such global judgements are influenced by many other factors than performance in one specific area. In addition to beliefs about competence in a range of (possibly unrelated) areas, self-esteem is also influenced by feelings of worth; clearly, these may be relatively unconnected to beliefs about competence in the particular domain we are interested in. As Kohn pointed out back in 1994, p. 274:

> [W]e can hardly expect an individual's general sense of self (e.g. 'I am a pretty good person') to have very much to do with his or her success on a mathematics test.

To recap briefly: while the relationship between overall or global self-esteem and attainment is unclear, more specific elements of self-esteem *do* appear to have a positive – and reciprocal – relationship with attainment. That is, improvements in performance tend to enhance self-concept, and the enhanced self-concept subsequently contributes to improved future performance. Such news is important for teachers. For those who were already committed to self-esteem as a legitimate part of their practice, based on concerns about personal and social education, it is welcome additional information to support their beliefs and their practice. But, for others who previously harboured reservations about self-esteem, it suggests that by enhancing self-esteem *in a legitimate and authentic way* they may actually be helping children to learn more effectively.

Of course, the key issue is how to enhance self-esteem in an authentic way, avoiding the mistakes of the past. The following chapters will provide advice on this, including the value of accurate and honest appraisals and addressing the ways in which children view their ability and their performance. But to conclude our look at research evidence, we consider some recent studies which have been conducted in primary classrooms.

The two-dimensional model: some recent research evidence from primary classrooms

In the light of these reviews of the research evidence, we cannot say that improving global self-esteem will lead to better learning, but we can say that enhancing more specific aspects of self-esteem – essentially *beliefs about ability or competence* in certain areas – may do so. A small number of recent studies which have used a two-dimensional model of self-esteem can provide further insights here. The three studies that follow relate to techniques familiar to most primary teachers.

Certainly, many readers will be familiar with circle time, popularised by the work of Jenny Mosley. This is a technique which is widely used and which claims to have self-esteem enhancement as a central feature (see, for example, Mosley, 1993). Despite the fact that many teachers choose to (or are required to) use this technique, Miller and Moran (2007) could find little evidence in the research literature to support the view that it does in fact enhance self-esteem. Consequently, they set out to investigate whether circle time has any measurable effects on self-esteem. They were also keen to learn whether an alternative approach to self-esteem enhancement – one based on developing children's sense of efficacy or competence – would bring about any gains.

The participants were 519 primary school children and their teachers, 21 in all, in different schools. Seven teachers were committed to circle time, seven to what we might call efficacy-based or competence-based approaches, with a further seven acting as a control group. (The efficacy-based group focused on emphasising achievement and recognising improvement.) The experiment ran over a term, with children's self-esteem measured before and after the experiment. Gains in self-esteem were found for both the circle time and the efficacy-based groups, but not for the control group. But what was particularly interesting was that the scores for self-worth and self-competence differed in the two groups which showed improvement, suggesting that the two approaches achieved their effects in different ways.

The findings indicated that circle time methodology (which essentially focuses on the creation of a climate in which individuals are respected and valued) helped children to develop a sense of self-worth. It had much less effect on beliefs about competence. On the other hand, an efficacy-based approach, which tends to focus on the achievement of learning goals, was more likely to develop the self-competence dimension. It is important to bear in mind that this was just one – relatively small-scale – study; in terms of evidence, it is very different to the large-scale reviews discussed at the start of this chapter. However, once again, it suggests that we need to look beyond overall judgements of self-esteem. It also points to ways of enhancing feelings of worth and judgements about competence.

Another recent classroom investigation looked at techniques of formative assessment. These techniques and strategies will be very familiar to many primary school teachers, who will know of the important work of Paul Black and Dylan Wiliam (2001). They demonstrated in 1998 that formative assessment could bring about significant improvements in learning. It has also been claimed that such techniques will enhance self-esteem and motivation; however, the evidence here is limited. Miller and Lavin (2007) set out to investigate whether formative assessment techniques do in fact influence primary children's self-perceptions, including self-esteem.

They worked with 370 children (aged 10–12) and 16 teachers. The teachers employed a range of well-known formative assessment techniques in the course of their day-to-day teaching over a six-month period. Information was gathered using standardised self-esteem measures, individual interviews and group discussions. The findings pointed towards improvements in children's self-perceptions in several areas. Specifically in relation to self-esteem, gains were seen in both worth and competence. Although there were differences related to ability and gender, the key driver seemed to be enhanced beliefs about competence, based on evidence of improved performance. Interestingly, gains in self-competence were most notable amongst those who had initially lacked confidence in their ability.

The third example relates to one form of peer learning – specifically, peer tutoring in reading, often known as paired reading (PR). PR itself has been extensively researched, and its value in many areas is well established. Benefits include improvements in key reading skills, as well as potential gains in self-esteem. However, as most teachers know, children who take on the role of tutor and tutee have different experiences. Miller, Topping and Thurston (2010) were interested in learning more about this, and in particular whether feelings of worth or judgements of competence – or both – were affected when children take on different roles in the paired-reading process.

The participants were children from 12 classes in different primary schools; four classes were involved in same-age PR (where children tutored their classmates), four classes were involved in cross-age PR (where children tutored younger children), and four classes did no PR and acted as a control group. The trial period was 15 weeks, with children following a very structured PR process. Children's reading ability improved over the period of the study, and significant gains were found in measured self-esteem. These were driven mainly by beliefs about competence. They were found in both the same-age and cross-age conditions, but not in the control group. This again seems consistent with a view which says that improved performance leads to gains in self-competence. Interestingly though, in the cross-age group – but not in the same-age group – additional improvements were seen in self-worth. It would appear that being asked to take on a role where one helps younger children can influence feelings of worth. At this point, some knowing teachers and thoughtful students may be nodding their heads; their experience has alerted them to this phenomenon. We return to this in later chapters where we discuss classroom techniques.

To summarise: these recent studies provide further pointers to the links between learning and self-esteem. Although they are on a relatively small scale, they have the advantage of *ecological validity*; that is, they reflect the reality of current practice in many primary school classrooms. As a consequence, they allow teachers some insights into the relationship between familiar classroom processes and self-esteem.

Some guiding principles for teachers and schools

At this point, let us take stock. From earlier chapters, we have learned that there have been many different ways of conceptualising and investigating self-esteem. One of the central issues is whether self-esteem is best viewed as a unidimensional concept – a generalised 'feel-good factor' – or a set of judgements which have hierarchical relationships with each other. In this chapter, we have seen that the latter model points to some elements of self-esteem (specifically in the area of academic self-concept) having a reciprocal relationship with school performance. In short, improvements in self-perceptions in a given domain contribute to improved performance in that domain.

For many, this is encouraging news, but we need to remember that these are essentially beliefs about ability or *competence* in specific subjects or domains. As the previous chapter alerted us, beliefs about competence are not the complete story; an individual's self-esteem is influenced by feelings of worth as well as beliefs about competence. It is not immediately clear where the dimension of self-worth is reflected in the differentiated model, and this leads us to the studies which have employed a two-dimensional measure of self-esteem. We summarised a number of these, which support the view that competence and worth are related to different aspects of classroom life.

So, what are the implications for teachers which emerge from the evidence in this area? A key principle follows on from the previous point: when trying to influence self-esteem in classrooms, it is more helpful to look at self-worth and self-competence separately. Although they are both important for healthy self-esteem, they tend to be influenced by different processes and they have different relationships with performance. Classroom experiences which influence one dimension may have little or no effect on the other.

We know that a person's judgements of self-competence are essentially dependent upon demonstrating to themselves (and others) that they can meet the challenges that they face. Stated very simply, beliefs about competence in a given domain stem from experiences of success in that domain. From a teacher's point of view, providing opportunities to succeed, structuring these to ensure an appropriate degree of challenge, having high expectations, motivating, supporting and sometimes cajoling pupils to persevere, helping them to appreciate their achievements and to set their sights yet higher, are all likely to encourage feelings of competence. To an extent, they *may* – but do not *necessarily* – influence self-worth as well.

In contrast, feelings of worth are likely to be enhanced by messages that affirm a child's value as an individual, *irrespective of* their levels of competence or attainment. Self-worth involves being accepted for the sort of person you are. It may reflect what we call character traits: the beliefs and values you hold, reflected in the way you live your life. Such characteristics are seen in the way you relate to others, showing care and compassion, demonstrating through attitudes and behaviours that you are trying to live by a 'good' set of principles. Where feelings of competence are driven by success or failure in meeting challenges, self-worth is influenced by messages received from others that you are accepted or rejected, liked or disliked and whether your behaviour is admired or disapproved of. Of course, such messages abound in classrooms and the teacher has a key moderating role here.

There seems little justification, either theoretical or empirical, for believing that affirming messages designed to enhance feelings of worth will have any effect on self-competence – and thus on academic performance. (This is consistent with the evidence we looked at earlier in this chapter.) But, of course, this does not make them any less important. Indeed, in terms of quality of life and mental health – of both individuals *and* society – they are vital. Further, given the nature of modern life, some might argue that they are more important now than in the past. Martin Covington (2001) is not the only person to point out that in today's competitive society, a person's value is often seen to be based entirely on their achievements. For those who are genuinely interested in self-esteem, this is a concern.

The preceding paragraphs may beg many questions – not least about how a busy teacher can organise teaching and learning to take account of all of these important ideas. In the following chapters, we develop these themes and provide more specific advice on processes involved.

〰️ Points to consider

Thinking about how you have worked to enhance self-esteem in the past:
- What techniques or strategies have you employed?
- How successful do you feel these have been?
- What makes you think this?

(Continues)

(Continued)

Thinking about the reciprocal effects model (REM):

- To what extent does your own experience tie in with the key idea that improving beliefs about competence in one area can help improve subsequent performance in that area?
- Can you think of examples which support the model – or call it into question?

What are your views on the importance of the teacher's role in enhancing both self-competence *and* self-worth?

- Are they equally important – for individuals, for communities?
- What reasons would you give for your answer?
- To what extent have you differentiated self-worth and self-competence when thinking about self-esteem enhancement in your class?

Thinking about the issues raised in this chapter, including the research evidence:

- In what ways (if at all) has your thinking been changed?
- What do you now need to know?

Chapter summary and overview of the following chapters

Many debates surround the place of self-esteem in the school curriculum. In the past, some of the more extreme strategies employed in schools have attracted considerable criticism, and opinion is still divided on the importance and value of self-esteem enhancement in schools. While many teachers, particularly in primary education, see the nurturing of self-esteem as a central part of their role, many others – together with some social commentators and politicians – remain critical of what they see as an over-emphasis on self-esteem.

The research evidence in this area is mixed, with different messages emerging from different studies. While links between global self-esteem and school performance are weak and inconsistent, those between more specific aspects of self-esteem (such as academic self-concept) and performance are clear. Research by Marsh and others points to the reciprocal effects of self-perceptions and performance (for example, Marsh and Craven, 2006). That is, improved performance in maths (for example) contributes to an improved mathematical self-concept; these improved beliefs about competence in maths can then contribute to further improvements in maths performance in the future, and so a reinforcing cycle is established. Taken together, the evidence suggests that global self-esteem and more specific aspects of self-esteem have different relationships with performance. This is consistent with a view that sees beliefs about competence and feelings of worth as having different relationships with performance.

A small number of classroom-based studies using a two-dimensional model have moved us further along this line of thought. Certain classroom experiences may help children to develop a sense of competence, but may not necessarily influence self-worth; other experiences may enhance feelings of worth, without affecting beliefs about competence. We can use this knowledge to plan classroom activities which are more likely to help enhance the self-esteem of the children in our classes.

The following chapters

Chapters 5 and 6 focus on strategies designed to enhance self-competence, essentially through supporting and recognising achievement. These are not based on quick fixes or superficially appealing commercial materials, but on improving key aspects of day-to-day teaching and learning. Such processes include effective differentiation, creating tasks which allow a sense of control, the use of formative assessment techniques, the potential of game-based learning, and the benefits of various forms of peer learning. Central to the change process is helping children to develop positive mindsets. This involves looking at the beliefs and attitudes we promote, and key ideas here include changing children's views of ability and learning. Importantly, we also look at the use of contingent praise and teacher expectations.

Following on from the chapters on competence, Chapters 7 and 8 focus on nurturing self-worth. Central to this is the role of the teacher, including teacher modelling. Once again, we revisit the complex issue of praise, making a distinction between contingent praise and messages of affirmation. This distinction is important when considering self-worth and we discuss classroom activities which have the potential to enhance that aspect. Key ideas here include the notion of 'required helpfulness' (where children are placed in situations in which others expect help from them), involving children in decision-making processes and giving them increased responsibility. We also look at classroom techniques and activities, many of which are already familiar to most teachers, to consider how they can impact on feelings of worth. These include circle time, other activities in established areas of the curriculum such as Citizenship and Global Studies, and one specific aspect of peer-assisted learning, peer tutoring.

Further reading 📖

1. For more on the wider aspects of the self-esteem debate, see:
- Covington, M.V. (2001) The science and politics of self-esteem: schools caught in the middle. In T.J. Owens, S. Stryker & N. Goodman (eds) *Extending Self-Esteem Theory and Research*. New York: Cambridge University Press.
- McLean, A. (2001) Have we got it wrong about self-esteem? *Times Educational Supplement Scotland*, 16 March.
2. More about the evidence on self-esteem and learning can be found in the following articles:
- Baumeister, R.F., Campbell, J.D., Krueger, J.I. & Vohs, K.D. (2003) Does high self-esteem cause better performance, interpersonal success, happiness or healthier lifestyles? *Psychological Science in the Public Interest*, 4 (1), 1–44.
- Marsh, H.W. & Craven, R.G. (2006) Reciprocal effects of self-concept and performance from a multidimensional perspective. *Perspectives on Psychological Science*, 1 (2), 133–66.
3. For studies in primary schools which used a two-dimensional model to investigate classroom processes and their effect on self-esteem, see:
- Miller D.J. & Lavin, F.M. (2007) 'But now I feel I want to give it a try': formative assessment, self-esteem and a sense of competence. *The Curriculum Journal*, 18 (1), 3–25.
- Miller, D.J. & Moran, T.R. (2007) Theory and practice in self-esteem enhancement: circle-time and efficacy-based approaches – a controlled evaluation. *Teachers and Teaching: Theory and Practice*, 13 (6), 601–15.
- Miller, D.J., Topping, K.J. & Thurston, A. (2010) Peer tutoring in reading: the effects of role and organization on two dimensions of self-esteem. *British Journal of Educational Psychology*, 80, 417–33.
4. For articles which have related the two-dimensional model to other aspects of school life (childhood resilience and primary–secondary transition), see:
- Jindal-Snape, D. & Miller D.J. (2008) A challenge of living? Understanding the psycho-social processes of the child during primary–secondary transition through resilience and self-esteem theories. *Educational Psychology Review*, 20 (3), 217–36.
- Miller, D.J. & Daniel, B. (2007) Competent to cope, worthy of happiness? How the duality of self-esteem can inform a resilience-based classroom environment. *School Psychology International*, 28 (5), 605–22.

5

Developing Competence: Some Classroom Techniques

Key ideas in this chapter

Until this point, we have focused on what we can learn from self-esteem theory and research to help our understanding. We have looked at the complexity of the topic, the variety of different perspectives on the self and the insights offered by different theories in the area. We have argued that what is needed is a unifying model of self-esteem, capable of providing a clear sense of direction for teachers. We have suggested that the two-dimensional model goes some way to providing that. We move on now to consider ways to translate this new understanding into classroom practice.

In this chapter, and in those that follow, our focus shifts from the general to the specific. We use insights from theory and research to guide our attempts to encourage a sense of competence and worth in children. We start with the first of these, highlighting strategies to enhance self-esteem through developing a sense of self-competence:

- strategy 1: employing effective differentiation in the classroom
- strategy 2: using formative assessment techniques to help build self-competence

(Continues)

(Continued)
- **strategy 3: exploring the potential of peer learning**
- **strategy 4: looking at the possibilities opened up by the use of ICT**
- **strategy 5: using game-based learning to boost performance**
- **strategy 6: looking for tasks which allow a sense of control.**

Introduction

It will be recalled from the previous chapter that a sense of self-competence is essentially the belief that one is capable of tackling the challenges one faces in life. It follows that teachers can help children develop a sense of self-competence if they provide opportunities for them to succeed. But, lest alarm bells are sounding for some readers, we wish to emphasise two messages very explicitly. First, the important word in the definition of self-competence above is *challenge*. We are not in favour of lowering academic demands – quite the reverse in fact; a genuine sense of competence is *not* developed by giving children work that is 'easy'. A challenge is not a challenge if it doesn't require effort. Second, we do not believe in *ensuring* success; children must be allowed to fail, for both personal and learning reasons. Failure is part of life and children have to learn to (and be helped to) cope with it and benefit from it. It is also an integral (and invaluable) part of the learning process.

Of course, failure becomes a problem when it becomes too frequent, or when it is seen as a source of shame, or both. If this happens, failure can indeed become damaging to self-competence (and also to the other aspect of self-esteem, self-worth). Indeed, one might reasonably argue that such a situation can become toxic. However, from the teacher's point of view, both scenarios are avoidable; failure should not be frequent, nor should it be a source of shame or guilt.

There is a world of difference between, on the one hand, *creating opportunities* for achievement based on genuine challenges and, on the other, manufacturing an illusion of achievement by outlawing failure. The guiding principle here is to create opportunities for children to achieve in the context of meaningful challenges and, further, to provide the structure and support to maximise the likelihood of this happening. This straightforward perspective guides the advice in this chapter.

It is likely that readers will recognise many of the techniques here, since they are essentially aspects of good classroom practice. What may not have been so obvious in the past are the links with raising self-esteem, through developing a sense of self-competence.

Strategy 1: employing effective differentiation in the classroom

We have already established that developing a sense of self-competence comes from feeling that one is capable of dealing with life's challenges. At the risk of oversimplification, a child who has a history of failure is likely to feel less confident than a child who has a history of success behind her. It will come as no surprise to hear that in order to develop self-competence in children, teachers need to create tasks which are challenging but achievable. We know that learners need time for reinforcement and consolidation, and for most children the increased confidence that comes with this is likely to enhance self-belief. A skilful teacher knows when consolidation and practice are necessary to embed a new skill before moving on. What follows is not an attempt to downplay the practice activities which are an important part of learning. But the drive to enhance self-competence essentially needs a forward-looking perspective; it should involve new skill or new knowledge or new understanding. Confidence in facing new challenges comes with success at doing just that.

This is where differentiation comes in. The learning experiences we provide for children need to be matched to their needs in order to increase the likelihood of meaningful success experiences. Of course, there is also an issue of rights here; it is difficult to imagine that anyone would deny the right of every child to receive an education which is appropriate to their needs and ability. Differentiation varies pace, activities, teaching and learning styles and resources in an attempt to best meet the needs of the individual. For decades, teachers have used differentiation to support teaching and learning, but possibly without fully recognising the role that planned differentiation might play in the wider development of learners – particularly in terms of their sense of self-competence.

There is a variety of methods which can be used effectively to differentiate children's learning. The most common of these would be differentiation by outcome, by task, by support and by response. All of these strategies can be seen on a daily basis in classrooms, with varying degrees of success. For those who have carefully matched the pupils' abilities with the specific task, success can be quickly evident. Although the pedagogical skills can be complex and challenging for teachers to master, the benefits for children can be considerable.

Perhaps one of the most common methods of differentiation, although not always recognised as being the most effective, is that of differentiation by outcome. This simply implies that the teacher plans lessons which aim to achieve different levels of understanding or achievement for different pupils – dependent on their abilities – when working on the same task. This can often be used in subjects that traditionally are taught as whole-class lessons, for example Expressive Arts or Religious and Moral Education. The lesson is taught, the task is explained but it is in the completion of the task – and the outcome on which the teacher will make the judgement – as to whether the specific learning has been achieved for each pupil. Teachers may look for such qualities as length, standard, complexity, and so on. Of course, central to the success of this approach is a good understanding, on the part of the teacher, of her pupils' levels of ability and also of attitudinal factors and any barriers to learning they might face. For pupils to appreciate that they have achieved success, they need to know what it is they have to do. Only when they are clear about this can they begin to work towards success. This is where the value of formative assessment is seen, since one key aspect of this is the clear identification of learning outcomes and success criteria. We discuss this further later in this chapter.

Differentiation by task is frequently used when a whole-class lesson is taught and then pupils, sometimes individually and often in groups, are given an appropriate task to complete. At times, this involves the pupils working individually on the same group task; at other times, this could mean pupils working collaboratively on the task. For the former, the teacher will usually adapt the task by adding a more complex challenge for the more able pupils or modifying the expectations of the task for others. Again, the challenge for the teacher is to ensure that the individual pupil, whether working alone or within the group, is clear about the nature of the response required. It is important for a child's sense of self-competence that he or she is learning in an environment which is positive and encouraging, and which demonstrates that the needs of the individual and their achievements are being recognised. Teachers using this method of differentiation will have ensured that the task is appropriate for each pupil, appreciating what this can also achieve in relation to the self-competence of pupils.

In recent years, the nature and scope of differentiation by support has increased greatly. Twenty years ago, the class teacher was often the only adult in the classroom on a daily basis. Perhaps the 'learning support' teacher might make a weekly visit but this was often to withdraw pupils who needed extra support from the classroom. Today the picture is a very different one; most classes have frequent access to classroom assistants, support for learning assistants, volunteer parents and helpers – and, indeed, often children from their own class and from older classes in the school.

Teachers have become skilled at making effective use of these others in the classroom, working collaboratively to give pupils a positive and supportive experience. Peer support and peer learning have some very clear benefits in relation to self-esteem which are discussed later. In a classroom where other adults are used to help support learning, there are many issues for the teacher to consider. Central to these is the question of communication, with underlying principles as well as organisational issues being shared between members of the classroom 'team'. Certainly, it is important that helpers are aware of their dual role here – aware not only of the specific learning and teaching points but of the underlying principle of developing the self-competence of the learner. A central role will be to help pupils to recognise any achievement and to appreciate that the learning is a result of their effort. A useful technique at the end of a completed task is to discuss with the children what they have achieved, or to say what they feel more confident about as a result of the lesson.

For many teachers, differentiation by response is perhaps the most natural of all of the methods of differentiation, although it can be one many student teachers find difficult to use. For an experienced teacher, with a sound knowledge of pupils and their learning in class, this can often be intuitive. For student teachers at the beginning of their professional life, visiting a number of classrooms for short periods of time, it is difficult to have the depth of knowledge required of individual children to fully develop this strategy.

Consider the use of questioning during a class lesson; teachers will pose particular questions at varying levels and direct these to particular pupils. By following through on an answer, a teacher can ensure that the pupil is challenged to try harder, think deeper. Skilful questioning strategies enable teachers to ensure not only that the pupil continues to answer the question but that he or she achieves success. Following up by asking higher order questions, where the pupil is invited to elaborate on an answer or encouraged to speculate, or indeed where the teacher offers an opinion or provides further information, all help the pupil to feel engaged and attain a sense of achievement and competence. After all, if the teacher is showing interest in your thoughts, responding to your contributions by seeking more information, and asking you to tell your peers all about it, you must have something of value to say!

There are many other techniques which teachers can employ to help differentiate learning tasks in the classroom. For example, one which we have not mentioned is differentiation by resource. By this we mean more than just providing simplified worksheets for less able children; we are referring to a range of ways in which we can use learning technology, both traditional (such as books, practical materials or voice recorders) and more recent (such as digital technology), to provide extra support to help children achieve. It is beyond the scope of this book to provide detailed advice about support for learning in its broader sense, although that is clearly central to any attempt to improve achievement. There are many excellent books which provide more detailed information and advice on that topic. However, in a section which follows, we do look at one aspect of this – the ways in which advances in ICT have opened up possibilities for teachers to enhance learning opportunities for children.

When differentiation is effective, it provides challenge and maximises the chances of success, supporting learning and encouraging beliefs about competence. The concept of appropriate challenge is central to the development of a sense of competence. Pupils who are not challenged in their learning are unlikely to feel that they have achieved anything of consequence. They may not value the task and therefore not see that particular task as taking them forward in their learning. Although, at one level, they may have successfully completed the work, they may not recognise that as achievement. In the next chapter, we shall look at the mindsets of children who choose to cover up a deficiency in self-competence by trying to convince themselves and others that their own minor accomplishments are worthy of praise. Such children often prefer to do low-level tasks which they know they can achieve rather than face a new challenge where their lack of ability might become evident in the class. Many readers will recognise this scenario; they may also recognise it as a self-esteem problem.

To conclude this brief discussion of differentiation, we would emphasise that to build a sense of self-competence children have to recognise not only their success but also to believe that the task is relevant, challenging and appropriate. In short, they have to appreciate the increment in their learning in order to benefit in terms of self-competence.

 Activity 1

Jot down some of the techniques you employ to differentiate learning.
In the light of the issues raised in this section, can you identify any areas where you might be able to develop your practice? (This might be in relation to specific areas of the curriculum, in certain kinds of activities you set for the children, or for certain individuals.)

Are there any areas where you feel that the element of challenge can be developed – perhaps for specific children?

How might you go about this?

Strategy 2: using formative assessment techniques to help build self-competence

Formative assessment is defined as the process of gathering information about children's learning and its subsequent use to inform the next steps in that learning process. In this respect, it is often contrasted with summative assessment, which essentially provides data to define levels of attainment at a given point in time. It can be seen that formative approaches focus on the ongoing learning process, and it is here that we see the links with self-esteem. It provides learners with the information they need to improve or move forward in their learning. The information gathered from formative assessment activities also helps teachers to plan more effectively for the next steps in children's learning. (In this last sentence, we see the links with effective differentiation, discussed above.)

Although neither the concept nor the processes involved in formative assessment are new, it is within the last decade that they have achieved prominence in the educational systems of the UK and many other countries. A significant factor here has been the research evidence (notably that summarised by Black and Wiliam, 2001) which demonstrated conclusively that formative assessment does improve learning.

The gains in achievement they summarised in 1998 were amongst the largest ever reported for educational interventions.

Largely as a consequence of this work, there are few classroom teaching and learning strategies where practice has improved so much in recent years as the area of formative assessment. It is probably fair to say that the important work of Black and Wiliam (2001), Shirley Clarke (2001) and others has reached every teacher in the land, with positive effects on children's learning and the effectiveness of many teachers. One reason many suggest for the success of this initiative was the very practical nature of the advice given by Black and Wiliam (see, for example, Black and Wiliam, 2001). They believed that, on the whole, classroom teachers have neither the time nor the energy to take on board a new idea or strategy – even if it is an excellent one – unless there is clear guidance as to how that can be translated into practical techniques to be used in their classrooms.

Formative assessment, like most educational initiatives, depends heavily on how much teachers understand the theory of it and how committed they are to making the changes in practice to implement these in the classroom. The success of the formative assessment movement in schools is proof that if the ideas are well researched and supported with practical app-lications for use in the classroom, there is every chance of them having an impact and changing practice on the ground. Black and Wiliam's writing has concentrated on academic (as opposed to personal) gains from formative assessment, but any processes which are likely to improve performance have the potential to enhance self-competence as well.

In fact, there has been a belief in many circles about the potential of formative assessment for enhancing self-esteem, and the study by Miller and Lavin (2007) (described in the previous chapter) provided further evidence to support that view. Specifically, they reported how children's sense of self-competence was enhanced by using several of the techniques, and linked these to messages – related to both personal and learning factors – received in the course of the activities. It is to formative assessment strategies that we now turn.

Teachers use a number of activities which engage children in processes of formative assessment and we consider here some of the most common techniques used. Identifying clear learning outcomes for pupils is the most obvious starting point. In fact, Black and Wiliam are on record as stating that sharing criteria with children is the *sine qua non* of formative assessment (2001); it is vital for all techniques. Children cannot make judgements about progress if they do not know what they are aiming for; stated more simply, if you want pupils to win the game then they must know the rules. In the past, it has often been the case that we have taken insufficient time at the start of lessons to share with pupils what they are going to be expected to do and what they are going to learn. By being clear about the learning outcomes, pupils are more able to manage the activity. This means not just that the targets have to be clear to teachers; they have to be in language that the children understand. Shirley Clarke's (2001) work provides helpful information in this respect.

Allied to this is the use of higher order questions, discussed above in relation to differentiation. The use of wrong answers is also important here, with teachers opening up and discussing in non-judgemental terms why a particular answer or technique may be wrong. Teachers are effectively doing two things in such situations. First, they are helping to identify misunderstandings so that learning can be improved. Second, they are providing a message that mistakes are not something to be ashamed of; they can be good, since they actually help us to learn! We return to the latter point in a future chapter when we discuss classroom climate in relation to self-worth.

Other formative assessment techniques believed to help learning (and hence having the potential to enhance feelings of competence) include wait time and jot time. Often used in conjunction with a no-hands-up rule, such techniques allow those children who process information more slowly the opportunity to think about the topic under discussion and contribute more fully to the activity. Self- and peer assessment – whether in a rudimentary form such as traffic lighting, or later in a more formalised way with evaluative comments – provide teacher and child with information about performance which can be used to identify future learning goals. Another common strategy used is 'thumbs' or 'fist of five', both methods allowing pupils to self-assess their understanding of the activity they are about to undertake and to share this with the teacher. Many teachers use this strategy after the initial teaching of the content of the lesson to ensure that pupils are clear about the activity and are confident to begin. Importantly, these techniques allow the child to convey a lack of confidence or understanding to the teacher without fear of embarrassment – hence making it more likely they will do so!

Many teachers will testify to the value of such techniques – not least because they provide them with information about children's learning which they can use to modify future interactions. But teachers will also point out that they have to develop children's ability to assess accurately and honestly. Accuracy in self-assessment can be improved by the use of clear and unambiguous success criteria, written in age-appropriate language, which serve as the focus for the assessment. Some feel that the issue of honesty takes a little more work. Children can be encouraged to be honest in a non-threatening classroom environment where the challenge and excitement of learning is the main focus; the creation of such an ethos is of central importance. Some children may also need support to recognise when indeed they do require more assistance. Although this too is a challenge for teachers, pupils who are able to recognise when they need support, and in which particular area, develop an awareness of the control they have over their learning. This sense of control goes hand-in-hand with feelings of self-competence.

It is perhaps in the area of teacher formative feedback that we can best see close links with the potential to enhance children's self-esteem. As with any learning experience, the more opportunity that pupils are given to be involved in meaningful dialogue about their learning, the better their chance of understanding that learning – and how that aspect can be developed and progressed. Although many writers have pointed out the value of encouraging children to become self-evaluative, Black and Wiliam (2001) have pointed out that self-assessment has to be more than a 'dialogue with the self'; opportunities must be created to discuss the results of the process.

Black and Wiliam (2001) discuss how formative feedback can help all pupils, both the high achievers and those pupils who frequently fail to cope with the learning or the task set. In fact, it is the latter group that they suggest can benefit most. For these pupils, language which focuses on the learning – rather than on individual performance or ability – helps to minimise the negative connotations of failure. When teachers clearly identify achievable next steps and promptly discuss these with the learner, pupils are more able to consider the work they have completed and the work they have to do in a way which carries fewer threats to them; they see learning as a natural, ongoing process, building on previous experiences. This can help them to see themselves as having control over their own learning. As we have suggested above, this is an important factor in enhancing feelings of self-competence. Moreover, if children do experience a sense of control over their learning, we know that they are more likely to take risks and to try things they may have previously avoided due to fear of failure. Timely, honest and encouraging words from the teacher can help pupils appreciate their successes and so help develop beliefs about competence.

Many formative assessment strategies are based on peer interaction. There is much evidence that peer-assisted learning (PAL) – particularly when formally organised, as in cooperative learning or peer tutoring – brings with it benefits in terms of self-esteem; some of these will be discussed later. However, at this point, it is worth considering formative assessment strategies that encourage pupils to work collaboratively; one of these is the 'think, pair, share' approach. As the title suggests, this method encourages pupils to take time to think about an answer before sharing it with a peer. It is believed that explaining information to another person makes greater demands on an individual, bringing with it benefits in terms of feelings of accomplishment. A similar sharing activity is the 'walk about, talk about' approach, which also encourages pupils to consider an answer and share it with others. When the activity is finally completed, the pupils have had the benefit of formative feedback and support from their peers which will inform their future work.

Ipsative assessment: a key ingredient?

It is important here to highlight one assessment term which does not appear regularly in the assessment literature, but which is important – for two reasons. First, it seems central to many of the techniques of formative assessment. Second, it is a very helpful perspective to focus on if we are interested in enhancing self-esteem through the competence dimension.

This is what is known as *ipsative* assessment; it is essentially *self-referenced* assessment. This means that instead of a child's performance on a given task being compared to other children (norm-referenced assessment) or matched to set criteria (criterion-referenced assessment), her performance is compared to what she has previously shown she is capable of. It is very clear that such an approach to assessment, identifying individual targets and focusing on the progress made towards achieving them, is central to formative assessment. Importantly, the ipsative approach has a clear developmental perspective; it focuses on growth and individual achievement. Its currency is increments in learning; we believe it is these increments that build self-competence.

Activity 2

Create a list of the formative assessment techniques you use in class.

- Now identify how many of these have the potential to enhance self-esteem by encouraging self-competence.
- How can they be improved from a self-competence perspective?

We have briefly outlined the potential of ipsative assessment.

- Can you identify any assessment tasks which have an ipsative component?
- Are there ways in which you can ensure that the ipsative message for children is highlighted?

Strategy 3: exploring the potential of peer learning

For as long as children have been seated next to one another in classrooms, some form of peer learning has been taking place. Inevitably, children will talk, ask questions and share with one another – even in classrooms where this is not always encouraged. Many of us can remember a concept or a skill becoming clear when a friend sitting close by took time to share how they had worked out an answer or managed to master a particular skill. Today, teachers have a much more sophisticated understanding of what is happening in that learning relationship; we are able to see and sometimes measure the learning which has taken place for the pupil being supported. Far from being discouraged in the classroom, this strategy is often planned for by teachers to support pupils in their learning. The benefits of peer-assisted learning for these pupils seem obvious, but what can sometimes be less obvious (and may have to be pointed out to anxious parents) are the benefits for those who are doing the supporting by sharing their mastery of a concept or activity.

In fact, there is no shortage of evidence that the more able peer – the helper – benefits greatly from such tasks, both in learning terms and in relation to self-perceptions. Readers will recall some of the evidence presented in the previous chapter about this; they can also follow up the suggested readings to learn more. But a story attributed to Jerome Bruner illustrates the learning aspects nicely. He reported telling a group of college students about quantum theory, only to be met by blank faces. He realised they had not understood, so he tried to explain it more clearly. The result was again puzzled expressions.

He collected his thoughts and explained it once more – and realised that this time *he* understood it (Bruner, 1963: 89). The point is that the mental rehearsal, and the associated restructuring of knowledge into a form that can be understood by others, is cognitively demanding and a valuable learning experience for the individual. Those who teach also learn – and with this comes the potential for growth in beliefs about competence.

What types of peer learning are taking place in our classrooms and how can such interactions enable pupils to develop not only their understanding but also the self-competence dimension of self-esteem? There is a range of activities which come under the umbrella of peer-assisted learning. These vary in terms of several characteristics – size of group, age and ability composition of the group, the degree of structure built into the activity, timing and frequency of sessions, the use of reward systems, and so on. (See the further reading section at the end of the chapter to learn more about the variety of different organisational factors.) Currently, the most common forms of PAL are cooperative or collaborative group work and peer tutoring. Cooperative and collaborative group work can take many forms and, through a variety of initiatives, is being encouraged in many regions and in several countries. Peer tutoring is a common strategy in schools, particularly in the area of reading where it is often known as paired reading. It is also growing in popularity in mathematics, where it is known under its alternative name, Duolog Maths. We shall not provide detailed advice on how to implement these in classrooms; there are many excellent texts which do this very clearly and successfully and we have included some of these at the end of the chapter. Instead, in this chapter, we shall refer to some basic elements of peer-to-peer interaction in the classroom, since these are common to many PAL techniques.

First and foremost, PAL is a learning process and, like all processes, its efficacy will depend on the level of teacher understanding – both of the theory and of the practical issues. In addition, like most techniques employed in the classroom, the skills have to be taught; it is not enough for teachers to place two or more children together in the hope or expectation that learning will take place. The process needs to be explained; pupils need to understand what is happening and why. They need to be engaged with the processes and see the value of their role in helping one another to learn; it has to be seen as a process of mutual benefit. Children have to be trained in the roles and processes in order to understand what constitutes helpful (and legitimate) behaviour – and what does not. This ethos and way of working may take time to establish in the classroom, but the potential is sufficient to justify the effort.

Central to the success of the strategy is for children to see both roles – helper and helped – as positive. This is a message the teacher will want to emphasise, but it is also something that the children can learn at first hand themselves. For example, Topping (2001a) has argued that PAL can be used with all pupils in class in such a way that they are sometimes the tutor and at other times the tutee. The reasoning is that all pupils will have areas of strength and areas where they could benefit from support from others. As this strategy can be used in all curricular areas, inside and outside of the classroom, most pupils will be able to have the opportunity to take on both roles, to support others and have others support them. Allowing children to appreciate for themselves the benefits of both roles can help to establish the value of the approach in children's minds. This aspect of children being both tutor and tutee at different times has recently been further developed in a technique called *reciprocal tutoring*. This is a more formalised arrangement which provides some excellent opportunities for children to gain in competence through helping – and receiving help from – others. We say a little more about this below in the section on ICT in the classroom (see also Further reading).

Perhaps one of the important areas in PAL in relation to children's learning and enhancing of self-esteem is the learning conversation pupils will have with each other. When a teacher carefully pairs a pupil with another to offer support, there is an immediate advantage; the tutor is watching the work being carried out and can spot any errors quickly. The discussion which then takes place is likely to employ language and make reference to concepts which are familiar to the tutee – possibly helped by the fact that the mastery of that skill will be fresh in the experience of the tutor. Errors being pointed out by a peer may also be less daunting for many pupils than if the same point was made by the teacher. The benefits in learning for the tutee are obvious; he or she has immediate support in taking that particular concept or skill forward, thus enhancing beliefs about competence based on new achievement. But there are also benefits for the tutor.

The story about Bruner, above, illustrates the maxim '*in teaching we learn*' and this is an important process for the pupil in the role of helping less able peers (Bruner, 1963). His or her own knowledge will be subject to conscious examination and re-organisation, and possibly consolidated and deepened, by the process of supporting others. An incidental benefit is that those in a tutor role will also be very aware of their relative advantage (in that specific area), further enhancing their general feeling of self-competence. We have found that lower-ability children who have acted as tutors for younger children have benefited greatly in this respect. Some experienced teachers may not be surprised to hear this, and this particular form of paired tutoring will be further discussed in a later chapter.

What of the pupils who are being assisted by others? For pupils undertaking a challenging task without the assistance of a peer, if they are struggling with a concept or activity, the chances are that errors will be made, with resulting effects on success and self-perceptions. After all, the teacher cannot monitor all learning processes all of the time. On the other hand, where pupils are given appropriate and timely peer support, they are helped to understand the concept or master the activity. As a consequence, they also *own* the new understanding developed from this. They know that they are able to complete the task successfully and that the work they are submitting to the teacher is correct; this develops feelings of competence. It also provides the opportunity for teachers to offer genuine positive feedback, reinforcing the 'feel-good' factor related to completing the difficult task successfully.

When teachers who use this strategy successfully in the classroom plan for this activity to take place, they usually do so for the purpose of the children's learning and not for the benefits in relation to pupils' feelings of self-esteem. However, this is another example of a situation where examples of good practice can have more than one benefit and where a strategy can have more than one positive outcome.

Activity 3

1. Consider the PAL activities you employ in the classroom:

- List these.
- How successful do you feel they are in enhancing feelings of self-comptence?
- Are there any weaknesses or drawbacks?

2. Some key characteristics of successful PAL are:

- children believing in the benefits of the approach
- clear task expectations
- a defined structure (in terms of roles).

Now look again at the techniques you have used.

- Choose just one or two recent examples.
- For each one, consider how the above three characteristics might be enhanced.

Strategy 4: looking at the possibilities opened up by the use of ICT

There is much debate amongst teachers about the use and role of ICT in classrooms. At one end of the scale, there are teachers who believe that modern technology will revolutionise education. At the other end, there are those who see it as a distraction from meaningful teaching and learning, or who perceive dangers in the inexorable spread of the internet and computer games (see, for example, the Byron Report, 2008). Somewhere in the middle, perhaps, are those who feel digital technology is just another classroom resource, albeit an exciting and important one. Many teachers now integrate ICT into classroom activities as a natural part of teaching and learning, even if some remain reluctant to employ it fully, preferring instead to use it as a reward for good work or good behaviour.

There are few teachers, whether they are fans of technology or not, who would disagree that digital technology can be a very powerful tool in the classroom. In a traditional learning environment, paper-based materials tend to predominate, and (it is argued) the means of representation is usually limited to text and pictures, often based on some notion of the average pupil. This necessarily puts some pupils at a disadvantage since we know that individuals learn in different ways and at different paces. Digital technology opens up possibilities for learners by using a wider range of representations, and so providing more ways to access information. For example, children can learn via text, still or moving images, audio, animations, by manipulating material on the screen, and so on. All of these open up opportunities for teachers keen to enhance learning.

For our purposes, a question we must ask is, can ICT be used effectively to enable pupils to have more control over their own learning and development; can it empower students and enhance feelings of competence in their ability over a variety of learning situations? Many experts in the field of educational technology would answer a resounding yes to the above question and Alan November (2010) is one such believer. In his book, *Empowering Students with Technology*, November gives a number of examples as to how teachers can allow and encourage pupils to take control over their learning using computers and ICT more generally. He also uses the example of students writing computer programmes to highlight the fact that for the learner there is instant feedback to indicate when something is working or not, and 'a total lack of judgment' on the part of the computer regardless of how many attempts one has to make to get it right.

However, these issues can be considered in a much wider context than simply designing computer programmes. The idea of the computer being 'non-judgemental' is an interesting one. Pupils who are developing skills in an online task can take time to gain the skills, the mastery of the skills being much more important than the time taken to master them. This online learning tool also works well in some institutions with student teachers who are trying to ensure mastery of their own knowledge and skills in certain subjects that they will go on to teach. The opportunity to continually go back and try again is certainly empowering, and links can be made with what we know about mastery learning.

All of the above considerations come together to enable and empower children and to develop their competence as learners. Remember that for most of these 'digital natives' the use of the tool (i.e. the computer) is not a barrier to learning; it is highly likely that they are competent and very comfortable in using the technology. In addition, there are many pieces of educational software specifically designed to support pupils with particular difficulties. These adaptive applications help individuals to better access their learning, responding to the child's inputs with activities tailored to the learning task and often providing personalised feedback.

It is interesting that November appears to see the effective use of ICT in the classroom as more of a cultural shift in thinking rather than mastery of a resource or strategy. If we recognise that having a sense of ownership and control over learning is desirable, particularly in relation to enhancing children's sense of competence, then a change in attitude may be what is required of us as educators; in such cases we need to consider the bigger picture. Considering not just when to use the computer in the classroom, but how to use it, provides an opportunity to look at what we actually want ICT to help us achieve.

In the section on peer learning, above, we made reference to the idea of children taking on the role of tutor (the 'teacher') and tutee (the learner) at different times. Reciprocal peer tutoring is the name given to this particular type of peer learning; it is when children act as tutee in one situation and tutor in another. An imaginative and educationally valuable use of this technique is using ICT – more specifically email – to facilitate foreign language learning with primary school children. In a study recently published, children in a Scottish primary school were paired up with same-age peers in a Spanish school. The Scots were learning Spanish; their counterparts were learning English. The children sent emails to their counterparts in their second language and these were then corrected by the recipients, for whom it was their first language. The process then happened in reverse; messages sent were always in their new language, and were subsequently corrected by native speakers. In such a case, children took on both roles at different times and, importantly, learned about the value of both roles. For more information on this, see Thurston et al. (2009).

We believe that setting up learning activities that allow pupils to exercise a degree of control over how they learn – and to *appreciate* that they are in control – will build both confidence and competence. There are many characteristics of digital technology which encourage children to exercise control but we look at one particular example as an illustrative case.

Strategy 5: using game-based learning to boost performance

Children have been playing computer games for a number of decades now and teachers have been increasingly interested in how these can be used in schools. Many games are specifically written for education purposes; these are often known as educational software or e-learning games. In addition, there has also been increasing interest in how commercial 'off-the-shelf' computer games (sometimes known by the acronym COTS games) can be used to encourage learning in the classroom.

For many years, computer games were viewed by many in the educational field (and many parents) as a time-wasting, anti-social activity. 'Addiction' to these games was often the subject of newspaper articles and television debate and this, coupled with other concerns about the effects of programme content on attitudes, created anxiety in the minds of parents. The Byron Report (2008), mentioned above, was one response to such concerns. Although such fears are still prevalent in certain sectors of society, recent educational research has focused on some of the real benefits which youngsters can gain by engaging with digital games.

Although some teachers and education experts now recognise that learning can indeed be taking place when young people are engaging with computer games, many education programmes are not using these as frequently as they might. Perhaps one of the reasons for this is not psychological but cultural. This is exemplified by writers such as James Paul Gee (2003) and Marc Prensky (2001).

In his book *Don't Bother Me Mom – I'm Learning!* (2006), Marc Prensky tries to allay the fears of parents and teachers who worry that children who spend large amounts of time playing computer games are not learning skills or dispositions that can be put to good use in the real world. In fact, Prensky discusses a number of real-life situations, from medical surgery to the United States military, where experience in computer games is seen as developing important skills which can give learners clear advantages in their fields.

Prensky's work on 'digital natives' and 'digital immigrants' is now well known; our pupils are digital natives, having been born into the digital world, whereas teachers (in many cases) have had to adapt to the new technology and the new ways of thinking about it. This means that teachers often have to work much harder to get up to speed with this technology than they would with other learning and teaching resources. Teachers may also have to accept the likelihood that pupils will have a much more intuitive understanding of this area than they do themselves. Of course, this can be an uncomfortable realisation.

Gee (2003) has also highlighted social factors surrounding computer games. He argues that there is a 'culture' of game playing which is shared by enthusiasts. Gee calls this a 'semiotic domain'. Importantly, this is a culture – a set of beliefs, values and practices – which teachers may not share, or fully understand. A combination of such factors may help to explain why teachers, while realising the potential benefits to children's learning, find it another thing completely putting this into practice in the school or classroom. It is a barrier that needs to be overcome.

The arguments in favour of computer games include beliefs about enhanced knowledge and skills, together with improvements in attitudes to school and learning. Although the evidence in relation to these claims is not as extensive as some would have us believe, there are now several studies which lead us to be optimistic about the possibilities.

But why should digital games be so powerful? Many explanations can be found in the literature. Quite apart from the cultural issues mentioned above (for example, that digital games are part of the child's world), the educational and psychological literature provides many possible reasons. The games are designed in such a way that they appeal to the abilities, interests and needs of the player. One key ingredient is the responsiveness of digital games; the game responds to the player's actions by instantly varying the difficulty levels of the tasks, modifying challenge and support as necessary, providing feedback to the player to ensure engagement. Other factors include an explicit structure, in the form of clear goals and a set of rules to play by, and the repetitive element which allows for a sense of mastery of the skills involved. All of these combine to create feelings that the player is in control; we return to this at the end of this chapter.

Further reference can be made to a range of psychological theories to explain the attraction of digital games for children, but common themes from almost all studies into game-playing have been the motivational factors and the aspect of challenge. One concept often associated with games is the notion of 'flow'. This is seen in the work of Csíkszentmihályi (1990) and refers to a feeling of complete absorption or engagement in an activity: being 'in the zone'. Children (and adults) who are experiencing a sense of flow have a complete focus on their key targets, enjoy high levels of concentration and 'lose themselves' in the task, often losing track of time. Flow is usually accompanied by a feeling of being in control of the task. Quite clearly, flow is not limited to digital games – even if it is often discussed in such a context. There is value in considering this example of intense intrinsic motivation in the light of classroom activities more widely. Although a state of flow is not likely to be easily 'manufactured' in classrooms on a regular basis, recognising it when it does manifest itself, and learning more about the characteristics which accompany it, will allow teachers to learn more about how to engage children in motivational tasks. Such a perspective is central to encouraging the achievement which is key to developing self-competence.

As mentioned in the section above, there is a mounting body of evidence about the value of ICT in relation to the learning experience. By way of illustration, we look at just one, which makes links between the learning taking place in digital game-playing and children's self-esteem. Miller and Robertson (2009) started with two basic premises: that computer games can motivate children, and that there is learning potential in many such games. Their study focused on three groups of children: one class were given a 'brain training' game on a games console to use each day in class; one class used alternative techniques to facilitate 'whole-brain learning' and the third class of children were used as a no-treatment control group. All children were given a test of computation before and after the experiment, together with a self-esteem questionnaire. What was discovered was that the games console group showed notable improvements in both speed and accuracy of computation which were at least twice those of the other two groups. But, importantly for our current purposes, this group also showed significant gains in self-esteem.

It is important not to get too carried away with what was a small-scale project, although it is worth noting that a follow-up study, using several hundred children in a range of schools from across Scotland, found similar gains in speed and accuracy of computation (see Miller and Robertson, 2010). These studies also reported that the least able children often showed the greatest gains. The message here is straightforward: these digital games seemed to bring about significant improvements in performance – gains that the children were very aware of. It seems self-evident that, used carefully, the improvements in skill and knowledge can help children to gain in self-competence.

What can teachers do to take advantage of the situations discussed above to ensure that children do grow in self-competence? Stated simply, a key role for teachers is to be able to see the *learning potential* in computer games and other aspects of ICT. It was a teacher, not a multi-national corporation, who saw the potential of some popular computer games for improving arithmetic skills in a fun way (as in the Miller and Robertson study outlined above). Similarly, it was another teacher who saw the way in which another commercial game (Nintendogs) could serve as a contextual hub – the centre of a thematic study – in an early years class. In that particular case, there was evidence of increased motivation to write and enhanced social skills. In addition to seeing the potential in the game, and incorporating it into learning activities, there is one more aspect. From a self-esteem perspective, teachers need to help children – some more than others perhaps – to appreciate any improvements which are evident.

We discuss some important aspects of children's mindsets in the next chapter, but suffice it to say here that some children can have a negative perspective on their learning (and on themselves). Such children may benefit from the teacher highlighting the progress made. A development of this is to extrapolate from a current success, pointing out the future possibilities, or generalising to other work or challenges. This latter point was exemplified in one of the studies reported above, where many children, while having clear evidence that they had become much better (and faster) at calculations, did not fully appreciate that this was making them better at maths. This is an area where the teacher can use her knowledge of the pupils – and of their learning – to ensure success experiences do translate into increased self-competence.

> **⊞ Activity 4**
>
> Consider the ICT applications you use in the classroom:
>
> - List those you use most frequently.
> - To what extent are these incorporated into mainstream teaching and learning – and to what extent as a reward or choice of activity after 'work'?
> - In your experience, what knowledge or skills are developed through using these examples of ICT?
> - In the light of what you now know, do you think any may have the potential to develop children's beliefs about competence?
> - Could these be further developed – and if so, how?
>
> Thinking about intrinsic motivation, and a sense of 'flow':
>
> - What evidence have you seen of children being in a state of flow?
> - Can you identify any characteristics of such events? Are there any key messages to take from these?

Strategy 6: looking for tasks which allow a sense of control

It will not have escaped the reader's attention that in this chapter we have made frequent reference to tasks which allow children to exercise control over their learning. One specialist in the area of motivation in the classroom, Alan McLean, has talked about this in the context of self-efficacy (2003). It is important to bear in mind that what McLean calls 'self-efficacy' is intimately related to self-competence. He makes reference to the level of engagement typical of children playing digital games, using this to introduce the idea of the SEGA factor. He sees this as being central to the development of confidence and motivation in children. (The relevance of the acronym will not be lost on those who recall an earlier generation of games consoles.) For McLean, SEGA stands for Self-Efficacy in Goal Achievement. His argument is a straightforward one: effectively, achieving goals to which we have committed ourselves builds belief in our ability.

The element of control is central to playing computer games. Quite apart from the fact that the player chooses when to play, which game to play and at what level, he or she makes decisions about strategy and reviews and modifies these in the light of performance. He or she controls specific game functions and the selection of key components, and ultimately it is the player's skill and concentration that bear fruit. The rewards include the intrinsic satisfaction which accompanies success in a new challenge or attainment of a new skill level; this is the building material for self-efficacy. McLean argues that the more pupils develop this, the more they will choose difficult tasks, try harder, use problem-solving strategies and have less fear of failure. It is in these positive strategies, all associated with successful learners, that we see the potential for the development of self-competence.

Central to the success of such games is a range of factors which can in turn be used as pointers for us as teachers. Some of these were mentioned above in relation to game-based learning; they include the match between ability and challenge, and the receipt of immediate feedback which allows rapid adaptation to the situation and modification of response. These factors are not limited to games, of course, and we can see links here to earlier comments about effective differentiation: the task being matched to ability. We can also make links between the feedback aspect of gaming and earlier comments about formative assessment. Another link is that the game player's progress is essentially ipsative in nature, with performance being compared with previous achievements – and current performance being used to set the next challenge, with *just* the right amount of difficulty.

Finally here, we have really focused on encouraging a sense of control in relation to learning (in the sense of cognitive activity) but the principle can be applied to other aspects of classroom life. Possibilities for allowing children to exercise control extend to the way that the school day is organised and managed by the teacher; a key idea here is to encourage children to take more responsibility for their learning. Many teachers will be familiar with the concept of the *integrated day*. This was a way of organising children's learning in such a way that they had a series of tasks to complete while having a degree of choice in when and sometimes how to go about these. One of the key benefits was that children had to take more responsibility for their learning. This approach still has its advocates (as well as its critics) and we are not taking a specific stance on it; however, we would suggest that encouraging pupil autonomy and providing a degree of choice (where appropriate) have the potential to develop a sense of control.

Those keen to learn more about the value of creating opportunities for control may wish to consult Chapter 5 of Winstanley's book, *The Ingredients of Challenge* (2010). Although her focus is on helping more able children, the principles related to encouraging independence and self-direction in learning apply to children of all abilities:

The advantages of independent learning parallel those of deep learning, where ownership and investment directly affect commitment and eventual outcome. (p. 95)

Many readers may be able to provide examples of the ways in which they encourage children to take greater responsibility for their learning, seeing advantages in terms of effective use of teacher time, as well as in levels of motivation. Carefully managed, these have the potential to lead to gains in feelings of competence.

∿ Points to consider

Think about any tasks you set for children that enable them – or better still, *require them* – to exercise control over the nature of that activity. These may be related to 'work' (involving written tasks or not) or they may be related to social or organisational factors.

- What is it about the nature of the task that allows children to take control of the decision-making process?
- How might the teacher interact with the children during, or after, this task to emphasise the links with self-competence?

Chapter summary and conclusion

In this chapter, we have taken one element of self-esteem, self-competence, and started to look at ways in which it can be enhanced in the classroom. Essentially, we have referred to 'everyday' classroom activities, pointing out how – if well managed – they can contribute to enhanced beliefs about competence. It will be noted that we have not referred the reader to the plethora of commercial 'self-esteem building activities' but have focused on a small number of key teaching and learning skills – aspects of good practice, in fact. Readers will notice the absence of advice such as: ensure all children are winners, make each child feel special, prevent failure at all costs, have no-score games and avoid red pens – all strategies which attracted (sometimes legitimate) criticism from the anti-self-esteem lobby. One of the reasons for their absence is the fact that there is so little evidence that they work; another reason concerns the potentially harmful side-effects of some of these strategies.

Instead, our argument is based on a simple truth: self-competence should be enhanced by real and meaningful improvements in learning. Consequently, we have discussed how effective differentiation is likely to improve learning and how with this should come enhanced beliefs about competence; how the recent emphasis on formative assessment techniques can influence children's beliefs about achievements; how peer learning provides many opportunities for children to appreciate how they can learn with and from each other; and how ICT, including game-based learning, holds potential for children to learn and apply certain skills more effectively. In all of these, we see some common threads: an element of learner control, the role of motivational learning tasks incorporating realistic challenge, and an emphasis on authentic achievements. In the next chapter, we shall look again at self-competence, focusing this time on issues such as the mindsets of children in relation to themselves and learning. Meanwhile, we conclude with a summary of some key pieces of advice which emerge from this chapter.

Some important tips (you may wish to add to this list!)

Do	Don't
• Use differentiation in the classroom to ensure realistic challenges	• Give children easier work to avoid failure
• Learn more about the abilities and learning preferences of the children in the class	• Make assumptions based only on previous attainment levels
• Get to know the barriers to learning which individuals may face	• Assume that low achievers lack ability
• Improve your skills at differentiating by outcome, task, support and response	• Rely exclusively on whole-class teaching approaches
• Develop higher order questions to deepen engagement and encourage new learning	• Limit your questioning to checking on recall
• Investigate resources (both low- and high-tech) to see how they can help individuals – but evaluate them carefully	• Accept the latest ideas in an uncritical way – or dismiss all new resources as worthless
• Use formative assessment techniques to help build self-competence	• Focus on the summative aspects of assessment
• Ensure children are always clear about the set learning outcomes and success criteria	• Assume that children know what is expected, and what constitutes success
• Make time to discuss self- and peer assessments with pupils	• Allow self-assessment to become 'a dialogue with the self'
• Focus on ipsative techniques	• Compare children's performance with other children
• Use errors to help learning	• Ignore or downplay errors and misunderstandings
• Point out progress made	• Just assume that children will appreciate what they have achieved
• Help children understand transfer (of skills or knowledge) – how new learning can help in other areas	• Assume that the children will automatically link skill in one domain with other similar skills

(Continues)

(Continued)

Do	Don't
• Maximise the potential of peer learning	• See peer learning as a threat to teacher control
• Investigate different types of peer learning	• Limit peer learning to (unstructured) group work
• Provide structure in the form of clear goals and role responsibilities, and training in group-work skills	• Assume that children will know how to work effectively together in peer learning tasks
• Use opportunities for (fixed role) peer tutoring	• Worry that in tutoring tasks the more able child gains little
• For less able children in particular, give them the chance to tutor younger peers	• Assume that less able children cannot be tutors
• Investigate possibilities for reciprocal peer tutoring within the class	• Dismiss this process as being unrealistic or difficult to organise
• Investigate the possibilities opened up by the use of ICT	• See the computer only as a treat or reward after 'real work'
• Learn more about how educational software can help children by presenting stimulating material in a range of different ways	• Just rely on tried and tested software when more powerful applications become available
• Learn more about the opportunities which are opened up by electronic communication	• Use the computer simply for word processing and presentation
• Investigate applications which can help those with learning difficulties	• Rely on basic drill and practice programmes for less able pupils
• Investigate game-based learning to boost performance in key areas	• Dismiss commercial games as being irrelevant to real learning
• Investigate how games can become a contextual hub for thematic work	• See games as simply an entertaining add-on to more worthy activities
• Be aware of moments of flow or total absorption in tasks; reflect on the characteristics of these activities in order to identify key features and processes	• Assume that children will only apply themselves if extrinsic rewards are on offer
• Set tasks which encourage children to exercise more control over their learning	• Believe that teachers have to micro-manage all classroom activity
• Also consider the organisational aspects when encouraging autonomy	• Minimise pupil choice in order to ensure that all tasks are completed on schedule

Further reading

1. For more on differentiation, see:

- Johnston, J., Halocha, J. & Chater, M. (2007) *Developing Teaching Skills in the Primary School*. Maidenhead: Open University Press. (See Chapter 7.)
- McNamara, S. & Moreton, G. (1997) *Understanding Differentiation: A Teacher's Guide*. London: David Fulton.

- O'Brien, T. & Guiney, D. (2001) *Differentiation in Teaching and Learning*. London: Continuum.
2. For more on formative assessment, see:
- Black, P. & Wiliam, D. (2001) *Inside the Black Box: Raising Standards Through Classroom Assessment*. London: School of Education, King's College London.
- Black, P., Harrison, C., Lee, C., Marshall, B. and Wiliam, D. (2003) *Assessment for Learning: Putting it into Practice*. Berkshire: Open University Press.
- Clarke, S. (2001) *Unlocking Formative Assessment: Practical Strategies for Enhancing Pupils' Learning in the Primary Classroom*. London: Hodder and Stoughton.
3. For more on peer-assisted learning, see:
- Thurston, A., Duran, D., Cunningham, E., Blanch, S. & Topping, K. (2009) International online reciprocal peer tutoring to promote modern language development in primary schools. *Computers & Education*, 53 (2), 462–72.
- Topping, K. (2001a) *Peer Assisted Learning: A Practical Guide for Teachers*. Cambridge, MA: Brookline Books.
4. For more on the use of ICT, see:
- Ager, R. (2008) *Information and Communications Technology in Primary Schools: Children or Computers in Control?* 2nd edn. Oxon: Routledge.
- Condie, R. & Munro, B. (2007) *The Impact of ICT in Schools: A Landscape Review*. Coventry: Becta.
- November, A. (2010) *Empowering Students with Technology*, 2nd edn. Thousand Oaks, CA: Corwin.
5. For more specifically on game-based learning, see:
- Prensky, M. (2006) *Don't Bother Me Mom – I'm Learning*. St Paul, MN: Paragon House.
- Miller, D.J. & Robertson, D.P. (2009) Using a games console in the primary classroom: effects of 'brain training' programme on computation and self-esteem. *British Journal of Educational Technology*, 41 (2), 242–55.
6. To read more about Alan McLean's views on a range of factors related to motivation, see:
- McLean, A. (2003) *The Motivated School*. London: Paul Chapman.
- McLean, A. (2009) *Motivating Every Learner*. London: Paul Chapman.

Developing Self-Competence: Creating Positive Mindsets

> ## Key ideas in this chapter
>
> In Chapter 5, we discussed a variety of strategies which teachers can use to help children to develop a sense of competence. These strategies and techniques were based on theoretical ideas outlined in the first few chapters of the book. In this chapter we continue to look at developing a sense of competence in the learner, with a particular focus on children's views about themselves and learning. We consider children's perceptions of ability, performance and motivation. We also look at how teacher expectations and the effective use of praise can impact on the development of a sense of competence.
>
> In this chapter, we discuss the following aspects of practice:
>
> * strategy 1: challenging children's views of intelligence
> * strategy 2: employing contingent praise to build self-competence
> * strategy 3: understanding children's motivational mindsets
> * strategy 4: sharing expectations, and other messages
>   for pupils.

Introduction

The ideas we discuss in this chapter are quite diverse, but they have one thing in common. They focus on key attitudes and beliefs – of both children and teachers – and their role in enhancing children's sense of self-competence.

In order to improve self-competence, we effectively have to improve children's performance – to facilitate new learning – and try to ensure that individuals appreciate what has been achieved. However, the quality of any new learning is affected by the way the pupils *feel about* the learning process: what motivates them, how they view ability and intelligence, and their feelings about demonstrating competence. Teachers' views are also important here, not least in relation to what they expect from their pupils and how they understand and subsequently use praise in the classroom. In essence, this chapter is about creating positive mindsets. These will allow children to benefit from their successes *and* failures, and realise the extent of the control they have of their learning in the classroom setting and beyond.

Strategy 1: challenging children's views of intelligence

It does not appear to take much time for pupils – even the very youngest – to decide who are the 'clever' or 'able' children, and who are not. Many a parent will have been informed by their child in their first year of school who is in the top group, even if the teacher has not explicitly stated this! The notion of 'cleverness' becomes evident very early on in the educational journey. For many, the notion becomes embedded: the clever and the not-clever. Now, clearly it would be foolish to contest what is self-evident; differences in ability exist, and they are real. However, from a self-esteem perspective – and equally importantly, when thinking about maximising potential – there is a problem here. It is that some individuals have a set of beliefs about ability, learning and performance which prevent them from achieving their potential – whatever that might be. Clearly, it is important for teachers that such unhelpful beliefs do not go unchallenged.

One important thing that teachers can do is encourage children to see that intelligence – and, more generally, ability – is not an entity which is set in stone, but is something which can be developed through effort. Carol Dweck (1999) contrasts what she calls *entity* and *incremental* theories of intelligence. An entity theory emphasises that we have fixed amounts of ability; there is nothing much we can do about it. In contrast, an incremental view says that our level of ability can be developed, if we work harder and smarter.

While an entity theory might not be seen as a problem for able children, it can be a considerable handicap for those who see themselves in a different light. Less able children may be inclined to think, 'I am not clever and I never will be; that's why I have failed'. One possible consequence, of course, is that there seems little point in trying harder, because it will make no difference. On the other hand, children with an incremental view respond to failure more positively since they believe that with more effort the task can be completed successfully. It follows from this that we may be able to help children achieve more if we can encourage an incremental rather than an entity theory of ability. Many experienced teachers, we suspect, will know that this is particularly important with less able children. However, they may also add that it is not easy to change such beliefs once embedded!

Before moving on to what we can do in this area, there are some other beliefs that are related to this. One of these is what is called the *locus of control*. This concept can be traced back to Julian Rotter in 1954, and relates well to Dweck's work on self-beliefs. Locus of control concerns the extent to which individuals feel that *they* are in control of what is happening to them, as opposed to external events driving what is happening. Someone who has an *internal* locus of control believes that their success at a given task is down to their own efforts. Similarly, if they fail, they attribute this to their own actions, reviewing their own performance in order to identify the problem. On the other hand, someone who has an *external* locus of control tends to look for other causes of failure – for example, the task was too hard, the person judging them was biased against them, or they simply had bad luck. Again, we can see the value of an internal locus of control if we want to encourage children to persevere with a task and find ways to succeed.

A third point we would raise here relates to goal orientation; that is, how we view a learning task and the associated performance. It is often explained in terms *of task orientation* or *ego orientation*. Individuals with a task orientation complete a piece of work because they want to become as good at it as possible: their aim is to learn more. If they fail in some way, this is not a significant problem since their ego is not dependent upon the success; they can try again to attain the mastery they seek. In contrast, those with an ego orientation are driven to out-perform others, since their ego or status is tied up with recognition; they wish to demonstrate or 'prove' competence. Such people can become disillusioned with failure, since it has an effect on their ego. There is also evidence to suggest that they will choose easy tasks in order to demonstrate their 'ability', and will avoid more challenging tasks because of the threat of failure. It is interesting to relate this to the defensive self-esteem behaviour discussed in Chapter 3 in relation to Mruk's (1999) model. Not for the first time, we can see some common themes in many of these theories.

The body of work on goal orientation is rather more complex than this short summary would suggest. We have been selective in our focus and those keen to learn more may wish to consult the Further reading section at the end of the chapter. But, for our purposes, this work – on children's views of ability, locus of control and task and ego orientation – points to the importance of knowing more about the ways in which children *see* the process of learning. Ideally, we would like to help children to adopt an incremental view of intelligence, develop an internal locus of control, and have a task orientation to learning tasks. Given the practical focus of this chapter, we now have to ask, what can teachers do to encourage children to have these positive mindsets about themselves and learning? We can look at organisational factors, task-based techniques and interaction between teacher and pupils.

Organisational factors and the question of grouping

In an earlier chapter, we mentioned the natural human tendency for social comparison – the tendency to compare ourselves with others. Signs of the ability of pupils in the class can appear obvious to their peers; a new reading book, more sums, harder sums or first work in the 'finished tray' can all be indicators to pupils of their ability and the ability of others in the class. By grouping pupils for very sound organisational reasons, we can mark some groups of children out from others. Given that organisational patterns tend to be regular, and groupings fairly static, it is understandable that pupils begin to connect these features with ability and therefore see ability as fixed.

One might think that the educational system has come a long way since a rigid adherence to ability as the sole organising principle. However, teachers still work predominantly with groups of pupils which are often, but not always, decided on the teacher's assessment of the pupils' ability. This is particularly the case in primary schools in subjects such as maths and language, and one can see the sense of this in terms of effective differentiation and good use of teacher time. The issue then becomes, do the children have to remain in these groups for other subjects? If we accept that there may be some value in breaking down a belief that ability is fixed, perhaps there is value in varying groupings where possible.

It is well known by teachers that groups can be formed in a variety of ways, including mixed ability, social groupings, and so on. Increasingly, the focus on collaborative group work and other types of peer learning encourages us to consider a variety of grouping arrangements. However, it is not unknown for teachers to go with the assessment of the previous class teacher and maintain the groups which worked together the previous year. Such experiences may reinforce fixed views of ability. But if we want to maximise children's potential by challenging entity beliefs about ability, this is more likely to happen in a fluid environment which allows for frequent and regular movement between groups. In such a classroom, children do not just see movement as a possibility; they have an expectation that this will happen. Of course, this will involve a great deal of flexibility in the organisation and management of teachers. (It also has implications for how such strategies are explained to parents.)

One justification for not moving pupils from one group to the other might be given as the de-motivating effect that this could have on some learners. However, in a classroom environment where clear and relevant tasks are set, honest feedback and praise given, and where pupils realise that they will move between groups often in the course of the year, then this is unlikely to be a significant problem. Of course, a big factor here is the way in which the teacher explains the classroom organisation and, in particular, the messages she gives out about the nature of ability and the process of learning. We return to this below.

Clearly, in some areas, it seems only sensible to have relatively stable groupings, particularly when learning is linear or sequential in nature. One obvious example would be maths. Teachers often group by ability in language too; while this may be useful for some aspects – such as phonics teaching in the early years – it may be worth considering whether different aspects of language learning *need* to be taught in stable, ability-based groups. In other areas of the curriculum, there may be many opportunities to vary groupings.

Discussion of language and maths raises the issue of the status of different subjects in school. For many pupils, and indeed for their teachers and parents, there is an expectation that we can and will learn in some areas of the curriculum, but also a willingness to accept children may not learn in certain areas. It is surprising how many parents will readily accept that their child just cannot draw or is not interested in physical education. There appears to be little expectation, or indeed for many any great concern, that there might be no improvement possible in this area. It appears that some areas are valued more highly than others by parents and this can surely have an effect on the attitude and progress of the child. Perhaps too there is a cultural element to this; Dweck (2007) cites the example of India, where there is a belief that everyone can do physics and so, on the whole, pupils cope well with this subject. However, in Britain, the opposite appears to be the case; it is seen as a 'difficult' subject that many struggle with.

If children fail to achieve in an area seen as important or valuable by teachers or parents (often language and maths), then naturally one might expect their confidence to be affected, even if they are skilled learners in other areas. Perhaps there are two issues here: one, that teachers and parents must be able to show they value all learning and two, that pupils are encouraged to recognise the steps they are taking (even where these are very small steps) in making progress.

Some task-based techniques

We have mentioned the situation with groupings; if teachers can make these more fluid, and remove the 'status' element associated with them, then they may be going some way towards encouraging more positive mindsets. What other techniques might teachers introduce to help in this respect?

Following on from the point about the relative status of different types of learning, one valuable technique is to encourage children to see *all kinds* of learning from incremental perspectives. This includes learning across all areas of the curriculum, but also what goes on outside school. Making explicit reference to children's hobbies and achievements out of school has real potential. Teachers can use these as evidence of increasing knowledge and skill; they can also form the basis of discussions about mindsets. Talking with children about how they become better at their hobby allows links to be made with school learning. One example concerns how we think about mistakes and failures. With a hobby or a pastime, failure to achieve something is often seen as a valuable part of the learning process; although sometimes frustrating, it points to a change in behaviour in order to get better. Children's differing conceptions of failure – for example, with a computer game and in a classroom task – can lead to some interesting discussions! They open up many issues which have a direct relevance to the mindsets we have been discussing.

One technique which has been very useful for many teachers involves assessment records – specifically evidence collected of children's previous work. Many primary schools now keep samples of children's work as they progress through the school. Such collections, known by a variety of names such as pupil portfolios or simply folders of work, essentially serve as evidence of progress over time. Periodically, these can be shared with the children to point to development in skills and knowledge, with an emphasis on how their ability has developed with time and effort. Children tend to enjoy this process, and looking for increments in quality in their previous work is a useful experience to emphasise development. Readers may recall the *ipsative* perspective discussed in the preceding chapter and see how this is emphasised; comparisons are being made with their own previous achievements – not with those of their peers.

Another technique which can emphasise an incremental perspective is the *self-evaluative footnote*. This is used at the end of a piece of work – for example, a written piece or some artwork – in order to emphasise development. The child will add a short comment to the end of a piece of writing, for example, to identify one aspect which is new: one skill employed for the first time, one piece of new knowledge which has been included, one characteristic which marks it out from what has been done previously. 'This is the first time I have written a rhyming couplet'; 'In this picture I have managed to blend the colours much better'; 'This is the first time we have done fraction sums'; 'I have put a lot of adjectives in this story'.

At the end of the week, children can look back over their footnotes, and use them to write a short self-evaluative *endnote*. The theme is, 'What has been achieved during the week?' or 'What can I now do that I could not at the start of the week?' Additionally, in the course of her marking, the teacher could reinforce some of these messages, or add to them. However, we would make the point that this process is not to be confused with the indiscriminate use of praise. The comments that the children make should be based on real perceptions of progress; the same applies to the teacher comments. This issue is picked up below when we discuss contingent praise.

Interactions between teacher and pupils

The messages teachers convey in the course of daily interactions form a significant part of the classroom ethos; such messages – both explicit and implicit – may be used to reinforce positive beliefs about ability, effort and performance.

When a child struggles with a particular task, the teacher will offer guidance and clues to scaffold the task. But, in addition, with one eye on processes of self-esteem, she might employ an *empathetic preface*: a comment which emphasises that there is nothing unusual in making an error or finding the task hard, and that it is a natural part of learning. She might start by saying, 'Yes, I used to find that hard when I was little', before going on to provide advice. Similarly, when a child makes a characteristic error: 'Yes, lots of people find that hard – come on, let me show you a better way.' Alternatively, 'I wasn't very good at that at first, and I thought I would never do it – but I kept at it. Would you like me to show you?' Such short prefaces supply a clear message; intelligence can be developed, and *even the teacher* had difficulties!

Essentially, the teacher is using two powerful social techniques to encourage an incremental perspective on intelligence. First, she is using her own life history; experienced teachers have learned that most children like to hear stories about their teacher's own experiences. Second, she is tapping into a powerful determinant of self-esteem: identification with models. It will be recalled from Chapter 2 that this is one of the main influences on self-esteem, with children identifying with their role model (in this case, the teacher).

Activity 1

Consider how you organise your classroom groupings:

- How 'fixed' do you think your pupils would feel they are?
- Which groupings (if any) do you feel *need* to be stable? Why is this?
- Are there any groupings which might be varied somewhat? What would be the challenges associated with that?

Thinking about the nature of interaction:

- To what extent do you try to reinforce an incremental approach to ability – either in terms of messages, or in terms of tasks associated with their work?
- Can you think of any ways to develop this?

Strategy 2: employing contingent praise to build self-competence

Lee Canter (in Canter and Canter, 1992) once famously wrote:

> What's the best way you can motivate your students? Praise. The most effective? Praise. What positive recognition can you give your students at any time? Under all circumstances? Praise.

Some teachers may still subscribe to such a perspective; others see in it the root of many problems previously associated with the self-esteem movement. Certainly, one might be forgiven for thinking that the issue of praising pupils is straightforward: pupils do something well, they are praised by the teacher. Being praised for a task will surely raise feelings of self-esteem. The problem is that this simple statement begs several questions; things are not quite that straightforward.

In order to enhance self-esteem in a meaningful way (and avoid the dangers which have fuelled the self-esteem backlash we referred to in earlier chapters), it is important that we develop a more nuanced understanding of praise. Several writers have expressed concerns about the use and misuse of praise. For example, some argue that praise is used primarily as a means of control, rather than as a way of encouraging children's self-belief and autonomy. It has also been argued that it can disempower children who become dependent on it. The wide range of issues related to praise is beyond the scope of this chapter, but see Smith (1999) and Kohn (1996) to learn more.

From the perspective of self-esteem, we can classify praise – or more accurately, positive messages – into two broad categories: contingent praise and affirmation. The former relates to praise which is *specific* and contingent (dependent) upon a product or a course of action. Examples are when a child is praised for a specific act, such as achieving a valued goal, acting in a certain way or completing a task successfully. It can be seen that this relates directly to meeting a challenge; from a self-esteem perspective, it is linked to feelings of competence. In contrast, affirming messages relate to comments, sometimes more general in nature, which affirm the child's value *as an individual*. Such messages may be less focused than contingent praise; they may relate to ongoing interactions and communications between the teacher and her class that indicate that the children are valued and liked for who they are, irrespective of their achievements. When a teacher shows that she is pleased to see the children, when she shares in their pleasures and achievements, when she empathises with their concerns, she gives messages that they are valued as individuals. From a self-esteem perspective, it can be seen that such messages are likely to influence feelings of worth.

One of the issues to consider here is that the two types of praise serve different purposes, certainly in relation to self-esteem. The wrong kind of praise may not work; it may be ineffective but, more than that, it may be counter-productive. For example, general messages of affirmation may help children to feel they are liked and accepted, but do little to enhance a sense of competence, since we know that self-competence depends on children recognising increments in performance. In fact, praise which is not related to appropriate achievements may have an effect opposite to that intended if it leads to complacency, or creates the impression that there is nothing more to strive for. Contingent praise, however, *could* help to reinforce a sense of achievement, assuming it was honest and allied to constructive advice.

On the other hand, contingent praise related to some aspect of performance might have little effect on the self-worth of an individual who is in need of affirmation; it may in fact make things worse. An example might help here. We may be faced with a child who is experiencing difficult circumstances which are eroding beliefs about her value and her entitlement to care and affection; traumatic family events or experiences of abuse would fall into this category. In such cases, contingent praise based on achievement may not address the problem; in contrast, messages of affirmation would be much more helpful. We shall return to affirming praise in a later chapter, but we focus here on contingent praise.

Even within the narrow focus of contingent praise, teachers must consider a number of issues before they can be certain that the praise they are giving will have the desired effect both on pupils themselves and on their learning. People react differently to praise. Some want – even seem to need – praise; they want recognition for what they've achieved, feedback about their performance, reassurance. Others seem to need little, if any.

Certainly, it is not the case that all pupils welcome the attention associated with praise. Teachers usually see praise as a positive thing, tending to use public praise as a strategy to encourage others to stay on task, or to behave in a certain way. This is consistent with current proactive approaches to behaviour management, with teachers focusing on desirable behaviour in the classroom rather than highlighting the opposite behaviour being displayed by another member of the class. Fox (2005) cautions that although it is an everyday part of interacting with others, it is not effective for all. For some shy pupils, this attention can be upsetting, and occasionally for older pupils it can be an embarrassing and uncomfortable experience which does not sit well with the 'cool' image they wish to portray to peers.

For praise to have a positive effect on pupils' learning and confidence, it must be given in a manner that they feel comfortable with. It is not just what is being said to the pupil, but how it is said. Often, younger children respond well to lavish praise and tend to take all teacher comments at face value. However, particularly at the top end of the primary school, for some children private compliments are more effective than public praise. For some older children too, an understated comment can carry more weight; it can seem more authentic than fulsome praise, which may be received with some scepticism. Once teachers can match the right kind of delivery of that praise to the individual, there is a greater chance that it will have an impact.

Another challenge for teachers is to consider the focus of the praise given to pupils. We can praise the work the pupil has produced or the manner in which it has been done. The latter tends to be more personal to the learner. We have already noted that for praise to have an effect on beliefs about competence, it should be specific to the task and a particular outcome. Following on from that, praise can focus on the product, the quality of the finished work, or it might focus on the *effort* the child has put into that task. This may vary from child to child and with the nature of the task, but there is reason to believe that for many children the latter is valuable; the individual is being rewarded for effort. It is clear that such an approach is completely consistent with the positive mindsets, discussed above, which we wish to encourage in children.

To reinforce an earlier point, many children find generic praise, given too frequently, meaningless; indeed it can have the effect of pupils ignoring all praise, even when it is genuinely merited. When is praise likely to be most effective? Like formative feedback in assessment, praise is most effective when it is given as close to the activity as possible. Praise can lose its meaning for many pupils, particularly the younger ones, when it comes so long after the activity that they can no longer see the significance. The learner can find making the connection between the activity and the comment difficult which can mean that it is not effective in relation to future steps in learning.

Side by side with contingent praise is of course encouragement. What pupils often need and appreciate whilst working through an appropriately challenging activity is support and encouragement to persevere with the task, gentle feedback and attention which helps the pupils to believe that they are able to succeed, that they have the skills and knowledge to complete the task. This encouragement can take the form of asking specific questions which lead the pupils to consider ideas that they may not have thought of, developing some of the ideas already identified by the pupils, engaging in discussions which allow children to think out loud and to test their theories and, importantly, allowing children space to have conversations about their learning. Such meaningful encounters can do two things. First, they demonstrate a real interest on the part of the teacher which is obvious to the pupil (incidentally influencing feelings of self-worth, discussed later); second, they move the children one step closer to completing the task.

In passing, we should note that we have focused largely on praise in the form of spoken messages. But teachers routinely use praise in their written feedback to children; the same principles apply. Many teachers will recall writing 'well done' on a page of work; the question we might now ask is, did the child know *exactly what* was good? As teachers, we are traditionally good at identifying problems, and offering focused feedback to explain the exact nature of the difficulty. Do we also offer focused feedback about what was particularly merit-worthy? From the point of view of enhancing self-competence, it is more helpful to write, for example, 'well done, you have remembered to put the speech marks around the words that were spoken', or 'well done, your cliff-hanger ending has really improved your story'.

To return to the main theme, McLean (2003) is not alone in suggesting that telling pupils that they are doing well in an activity when they are clearly very aware that this is not the case can do far more harm than good. Indeed, he suggests that a critical comment delivered by a teacher whom the pupils respect and know to be honest can be more effective in encouraging learning. If a teacher praises children in the class whether the task has been done well or not, or whether the learners have tried hard or not, it can be tantamount to telling pupils that nothing more can be expected from or of them. Indeed, the children may perceive that the teacher does not think highly of them as learners. Obviously, this is likely to have a negative – not a positive – effect on beliefs about competence.

This leads on to another point in relation to the use of praise; to be effective, praise needs not only to be specific or contingent (and take account of individual perceptions), it needs to be *proportionate*. If children receive praise which is out of proportion to what they have done – 'over the top' – then it can have negative consequences. Research has shown that learners who receive praise which is excessive in relation to their achievement tend to question the value of what they have achieved. Moreover, it can have a negative effect on their self-concept (for more, see Thompson and Hepburn, 2003).

Pulling all these factors together, we see that to be effective in terms of enhancing learning and thus self-competence, praise needs to be focused, contingent on performance (or effort) and perceived as sincere. It is important that the teacher has established an ethos of honest dialogue and feedback, as well as an atmosphere of trust and respect, for pupils to comfortably take on board the praise or criticism and use that to develop their learning or achieve their goal.

Activity 2

- In light of the issues raised in this section, identify some ways in which you can employ contingent praise in the classroom.
- Can you recall any occasions when praise has not been successful? In the light of the discussion above, can you think of reasons why this was so?
- What factors will you now take into account in order to make your messages more effective? These can be in relation to spoken feedback with children, written comments on work or other forms of interaction.

Strategy 3: understanding children's motivational mindsets

Obviously, a key aspect of the role of the teacher is to enable children to learn: to develop understanding of concepts, consider values and attitudes, and practise skills. Yet, although consideration is often given as to how we can structure that learning, frequently there is less attention paid to how teachers are going to help children *want* to learn. Those involved in teaching children of all ages know that pupils will learn more effectively when they want to know more about something or when an area or topic is of interest or relevance to them. We have heard about previously reluctant readers who are given texts about football or motorcycle racing and who are motivated through their passion for the content to learn to read the words on the page. How can teachers motivate pupils to learn? What can be done to make use of pupils' intrinsic motivation, their natural interest in a topic, and how can this be supplemented by extrinsic motivation such as rewards? Is there a link between motivation and enhancing children's sense of self-competence? If so, what is that link and how can teachers use it to best advantage?

In his book *The Motivated School* (2003), Alan McLean suggests that motivation has two functions: a 'direction function and an intensity function'. We might add to that an initiation function. Put simply then, motivation is about capturing attention, directing children to worthwhile activity and maintaining that enthusiasm.

While most teachers will immediately recognise the value of intrinsic motivation, perhaps the trend, certainly in primary schools in the recent past, has been one of focusing on extrinsic motivation, both in relation to good behaviour and indeed for learning. Classrooms up and down the land abound with star charts, pupil of the week, king or queen of learning, cubes in the jar, raffle ticket draws and golden time; indeed, in some schools children can achieve *shiny* golden time! The list is almost endless. In many cases, these may work to some extent, though not in all classes and not at all times. What is perhaps less frequently observed in classrooms is an ethos centred on intrinsic motivation. This is a much more difficult notion to pursue with pupils and therefore more challenging for teachers and school managers.

There are certainly teachers who are uncomfortable with the culture of continual rewards, sometimes rewards given for what appears to be very little effort or achievement on the part of the pupil. Following on from what has been said in an earlier section, this does not prepare pupils well for the world of work where this would certainly not be the norm. If pupils learn in a classroom where the teacher openly discusses motivational issues, then they may be helped both in the short and longer term. The teacher can acknowledge that it is natural that some activities will be enjoyable and interesting whilst others may just appear to be hard work. There is an honesty about this approach which we believe is beneficial both in personal and academic terms. By using the language of motivation with pupils, they will have a greater understanding of why some tasks are intrinsically motivating and why some are not. Importantly, such understanding can help children's perception of themselves as competent learners.

Pressley et al. (2003) make a very interesting observation and one many practitioners would recognise. They highlight the excitement and enthusiasm evident in children in the early years of their school life. What is more, most of these young learners believe they can and will achieve. Move up a few years and that enthusiasm, as well as that certainty of success, has often diminished. Whether this reflects many years in school where success has not always been achieved, or whether it just reflects a growing awareness of personal strengths and limitations which comes with maturity, the consequence can be reduced motivation. Success motivates, and pupils who are more motivated to learn are more likely to learn; that learning will deepen a sense of competence as a learner, and in turn may further increase motivation.

Pressley et al. also discuss the important role of the teacher in developing a motivational mindset in pupils. They claim that teachers who are committed to their pupils and who clearly demonstrate that commitment in their efforts to support and teach pupils produce pupils who are more likely to respond positively and want to learn. Again, it is easy to see the sense of this claim. As human beings, it is natural to want to please those individuals for whom we care and who show care to us.

In the last decade, the work of McLean (2003) has enabled teachers to give real consideration to motivation and the opportunity they have to harness that in the classroom situation. McLean refers to this work as 'motivational mindsets' and suggests that we can influence children to help them develop this type of disposition. It could be said that many classroom environments conspire against this kind of disposition developing in pupils. For many children, when they consider themselves as learners – something which they have to do on a day-to-day basis – they have to make choices about their learning. If a pupil is successful and in a classroom where a 'can do' attitude is promoted and where failure is simply seen as a building block, the pupils are more likely to choose to try, to make an attempt at the activity. If, on the other hand, pupils are in a class where failure is seen as confirmation of lack of ability, pupils are much more likely to find ways of avoiding finding themselves in that situation.

Both of these situations have an effect on the perceptions of self-competence of children. The former will have their idea of themselves as successful learners reinforced; in the case of the latter, pupils will have their negative feelings reinforced. For those children afraid to engage with the task, who seek to preserve what little self-competence they have, there can be little opportunity for meaningful learning to occur.

For some teachers, there is a hope – for others a conviction – that developing children's motivation through extrinsic rewards will lead to them developing an intrinsic motivation for learning. For others, this is seen as being unrealistic; all of us have a combination of extrinsic and intrinsic motives for our actions. Even in terms of learning, is it not the case that we are all intrinsically motivated to learn things in some areas rather than in others? It could be argued that the role of the teacher is to encourage and nurture intrinsic motivation while employing extrinsic rewards to support children in areas which may appear less interesting or indeed less manageable. Clearly, this points to a combination of both types of motivation, and work by Edward Deci and Richard Ryan provides a helpful perspective here (see, for example, Ryan and Deci, 2000). In essence, their work on what they call *Self-Determination Theory* (SDT) helps us to move away from traditional ways of conceptualising motivation – as simply extrinsic or intrinsic – and encourages us to look at a *range* of motives which individuals have for their actions. We believe it can offer important insights for teachers.

Figure 6.1 below is an attempt to summarise some important aspects of this theory. It can be seen that what has traditionally been labelled extrinsic motivation can be further divided into a range of quite different motives, or mindsets. In practice, this means that although I am not intrinsically motivated to tackle a task, I might have one of *many* extrinsic motives for wanting to do it. The point is, of course, that if teachers can learn more about the extrinsic motives of their children, they can use this information to help them learn more effectively.

Type of motivation	Extrinsic – different levels				Intrinsic
Child's motives for action	I'm acting to gain a reward	I want recognition for doing this – e.g. from the teacher	I value this – it will help me	This is important for who I am	I enjoy this – it is interesting and gives me pleasure
Possible progression for pupils?	···▶				
Nature of regulation	External	Introjected	Identified	Integrated	Intrinsic

Figure 6.1 An extended perspective on motivation

There is not scope here to analyse this model in detail, and we would refer the reader to the suggested reading at the end of the chapter. However, we would suggest that it can help teachers in their quest to maximise learning – and from this, enhance the competence dimension of self-esteem – by alerting us to the range of motives children may have in the classroom. We would finish with one very simple piece of advice in relation to this model. Reflecting the arrow in the diagram, it would seem sensible to encourage children to progress towards greater self-regulation in their learning: towards the right in terms of their motives. In short, we want them to move away from focusing on the rewards they may receive towards an appreciation of the value that learning may have for them. Bearing this in mind, it would be a mistake to introduce a strategy in the class which encourages children to move backwards towards external regulation. Teachers can sometimes do this unwittingly when they introduce reward systems (external regulation) when some – or many – children have progressed to the level of identified or integrated regulation. Given the current emphasis on reward systems, there may be food for thought here; once again we see how 'obvious' good strategies can have some potential drawbacks.

Although the work of Deci and Ryan draws our attention to mindsets related to extrinsic motivation, we should not forget the value of intrinsic motivation. A combination of research evidence and classroom folklore has provided us with information about the sorts of activities known to motivate children. These include the following:

Authentic tasks – tasks which are meaningful for children and relevant to their lives tend to 'strike a chord'. Experienced teachers know when teaching the topic of area to ask children to design a playground; or when working with percentages to task children with finding out the best discount on mobile phones; or when working with symmetry to design kaleidoscope images. They also know to link tasks to topical events and children's current preoccupations.

Manageable challenge – laying down a challenge is known to motivate children, particularly when that challenge appears somewhat difficult but ultimately achievable. These challenges can relate to individual performance in a particular area, or they can involve working with peers. The latter often involve *cooperation within* groups and sometimes a degree of *competition between* them.

Curiosity – creating situations which include a degree of complexity or uncertainty will naturally stimulate interest in children. Many student teachers will recall lessons during which the children seemed intrinsically motivated, often stemming from an initial stimulus which had an element of mystery about it. One wonders how many successful lessons have been built around a stimulus which has included vague or curious images, sounds which couldn't *quite* be classified, perplexing or incongruous artefacts, and so on.

Control – allowing children a sense of control is motivating for them. It will be recalled that in the previous chapter we discussed the value of developing a sense of autonomy; we mentioned both learning and organisational factors.

Fantasy – allowing the imagination full rein can help motivation. In imaginary situations, children can experiment and not worry unduly about the constraints of reality. Once more, the use of modern technology can help here, but there are many other opportunities to allow children to use their imaginations in conventional ways. Of course, one of these is in play. In fact, it is worth noting that all of these characteristics are present in play. For more on this topic, see McLean (2003).

Activity 3

- Using the model in Figure 6.1 above, look at the different categories in the row 'Motives for action'. Try to identify examples of your own motives for different actions at different points on the continuum.

- Does this model shed any light on how different children may see learning in your own classroom? What might be some of the implications?

- Reflecting back on particularly successful lessons, can you identify any characteristics which contributed to intrinsic motivation?

Strategy 4: sharing expectations, and other messages for pupils

For many decades, there has been a lively educational debate about how teacher expectations might affect the development and achievement of children. The debate was fuelled by the study reported in the book *Pygmalion in the Classroom* (Rosenthal and Jacobson, 1968). That study indicated that where teachers have low expectations of pupils, their performance reflects this; likewise, when teachers have high expectations of pupils, then the pupils are more likely to achieve. In the decades since that groundbreaking work, many of the claims and arguments have been refined and modified, but there are still teachers and educationalists in very significant numbers who believe that there is truth in these claims.

For government, local authorities and school governors, raising expectations can be seen as a very attractive – and obvious – strategy for achieving success in schools, and one can understand why. There is no financial cost involved in teachers having high expectations of pupils, so this strategy appears to be the perfect solution for pupils' achievement. Simply by expecting your pupils to do well they will. Of course, remembering the adage 'when something looks too good to be true it usually is', we recognise that there is more to it than this. Let us look more closely at this strategy.

When the notion of 'high expectations' is discussed, it is usually with children's attainment as the focus. However, for many experienced teachers, the idea of high expectations is a permeative one. There is little point in having high expectations of children's learning whilst having low expectations in other areas of their school lives. High expectations of achievement must also take account of standards of behaviour, of accuracy and neatness, and so on. Pupils need a consistent experience of high standards and expectations in the classroom; it is through this consistency that they will be able to focus on their own achievement and recognise their competence.

Of course, what might be considered to be a high expectation for one pupil might not be so for others in the class. Teachers have to be realistic in setting expectations. If the targets are so high that pupils cannot meet them, then the strategy will not encourage the pupils to learn and therefore it will not succeed; this is equally the case if the thresholds are too low. The comments made about differentiation in the previous chapter obviously relate to this issue. Through ongoing formative and summative assessment, teachers know what the next steps in a child's learning should be. Using this knowledge to plan challenging activities that push the boundaries, teachers can show that realistically high expectations can be identified for all pupils in the class.

An interesting issue though relates to teachers' values and attitudes, rather than simply their knowledge of children's abilities. Teachers tend to share a number of common values which are seen to be important in the learning environment. When groups of student teachers were asked to select the three most important values for their own lives and for their classroom, honesty, respect for self and others and equality were identified as being important to them as individuals; they were also identified as the values they would actively promote in the classroom with their pupils. However, teachers are human and amongst the practicalities of everyday teaching, there may sometimes be a gap between one's principles and values and the practicalities of classroom life. If teachers can remember that all individuals have potential which, when nurtured, can enable them to achieve, then these pupils are more likely to respond positively to the high expectations.

Regardless of the high expectations teachers may have for pupils, if these expectations are not communicated clearly to pupils then they are unlikely to have any effect at all. Teachers need to be very clear about the goals which are being set for pupils' learning. Only when these targets have been identified, shared and discussed can pupils begin to work towards them. But in fact there is more to it than this. Most readers will be familiar with the idea of the *hidden curriculum*: the messages children pick up which may not be stated explicitly by the teacher, but which children learn in the course of day-to-day life in school.

For example, what messages do children pick up when boys and girls line up separately after playtime? And when the teacher chooses girls to tidy up the painting area but asks for some 'strong boys' to carry a box of books? What message is conveyed when our own handwriting – or our desk – is untidy? What message is given when a teacher uses the threat of extra maths work as a sanction? To return to something discussed earlier, what are the implicit messages associated with the way groups are organised? What meanings do children take when one group appears to receive more of the teacher's time than others?

In reality then, teachers give out messages both directly and indirectly. It is not possible to look at all such messages here, but we can look briefly at some messages which have direct relevance to children's feelings of competence. These are the ways we deal with failure, how we appear to value children's efforts and the way we emphasise high but realistic standards.

Value added from failure

By this point in the book, readers will be in no doubt that we do not subscribe to the view that to improve self-esteem you should avoid failure; quite the reverse, in fact. We have given several reasons for this belief and there is no need to revisit them here. What we focus on now is how we can use failure as a step towards improved performance and, therefore, enhanced self-competence. This involves using mistakes and errors to identify and then rectify misunderstanding, within a context where direct, overt messages – and more subtle, covert ones – present failure as a positive learning opportunity.

First and foremost, failure has to be seen as a positive step, something that gives us a helpful message that we need to change something. Teachers can model this themselves: 'Oh, that's interesting; that hasn't worked. I wonder what we need to do to fix that?' or 'Right, this isn't going to do; I wonder what we can try now?' Such questions, asked in a positive enthusiastic tone, are forward-looking and point to benefits and opportunities – not defeat or shame. Lessons which are based on redrafting, reworking or improving products – of many types – can be an opportunity to emphasise that getting things wrong (or not quite right) is a step along the way towards something that can be better.

Teachers of a certain vintage may remember undertaking what are called *task analysis* and *error analysis*. Although these are different processes, they can both involve looking at what children have done in order to identify what has gone wrong: the element that has caused problems. It goes without saying that the more skilled teachers become at these processes, the more effectively they can highlight the particular elements that children need to work on. This will enable them to improve learning more effectively.

In fact, teachers can base lessons around error analysis – and use this opportunity to emphasise that finding errors is an important part of getting better. Another strategy that teachers can use to highlight a positive approach here relates to a piece of work which has gone through processes of drafting and redrafting. Children are asked what weaknesses or omissions they spotted in earlier drafts which *have been useful*, because they have allowed them to produce a better final product.

Valuing children's efforts

Teachers can give many explicit and implicit messages about performance by showing that they value what the children have done. At an explicit level, this relates to what has been stated earlier in this chapter about contingent praise. Stated simply, when praising some work, we should highlight those features which are particularly important. But, in addition, we give out many other messages about how we value children's work. Some implicit messages relate to whether or not we mark and return work promptly. If work sits around unmarked for ages, what does this tell the children about its importance? Similarly, a pile of finished pieces of writing, stuffed carelessly in a tray, gives a message about how the teacher rates the work. The same pieces, mounted neatly on the wall, give an altogether different message about their value –about what has been achieved. This can be emphasised by a caption which identifies some important features; similarly, if the teacher draws attention to them, it adds to the message. (It is also an opportunity to reinforce messages about neatness and presentation.)

It is perhaps an unfortunate aspect of the changes in teacher education that insufficient attention is often paid to the value of display in primary classrooms. We would argue that displays of children's work can be seen as an extension of the learning opportunities provided. Importantly, teachers can use displays to reinforce important messages about the processes of learning. The teacher can ask questions about what is displayed, children can talk about the process they went through, and the teacher can use the opportunities provided to emphasise messages about competence and incremental views of the learning process. Children can be motivated to emulate their peers, or to improve on their own performances.

Setting high standards

By setting the bar high, by expecting a lot of their pupils, teachers are effectively giving a message that they respect these pupils' abilities and learning potential. In turn, pupils who work in an encouraging but honest classroom environment will trust that the task set is within their capabilities and are more likely to strive to achieve their goals. Consequently – and this is central to the whole purpose of this book – their feelings of self-competence are more likely to be enhanced if they see themselves take on a challenging task and achieve a level of success. This is nicely illustrated in Carrie Winstanley's book, *The Ingredients of Challenge* (2010), where she quotes a pupil, Toby, talking about learning sometimes 'making his brain hurt' while he is doing it, but subsequently realising, 'Wow, I actually did that myself!' It is here that we see the link between achieving a *challenging* goal and gains in self-competence. If we avoid tough challenges through fear of failure, we risk diminishing – not protecting – self-esteem. So, a teacher who holds the view that all children can experience success, and who sets high standards, may in some part already be ensuring that her pupils are more likely to achieve success.

Apart from explicit statements, in what ways can a teacher communicate high expectations? One is by developing an ethos which says, 'doing our best in all things is how we work'. Reinforcement of that message at every opportunity will help sustain this – whether related to learning, conduct or attitude. Teacher modelling can also be a part of this. If a teacher shows that she sets high standards for herself, this can reinforce explicit messages. She can use stories about people who have achieved success in a given field; she can also use examples from her own experience. In both these cases, she can emphasise striving for improvement and the eventual rewards it brings. In addition, in day-to-day classroom life she can give messages that she is always trying to improve things. Such comments can also reinforce the message about doing your best at all times: 'The way I have set up this area is not quite right, yet; I'll have to make it easier for you to get your resources'; 'I'm sorry I didn't have time to look at all your stories; I am going to do this as soon as possible'; 'I am not really pleased with the way this has worked out; I think I can make this better for us.' Such statements, spoken with a note of calm determination, can convey a clear message: errors or failures help guide us and lead to improvement. Periodically, the teacher can explain or demonstrate how things *have* been improved: 'You know, if that bit had not gone wrong, we wouldn't have found out about this *better* way!' Providing they are used to improve learning, mistakes lead to successes.

We conclude this section with one final point in relation to realistic expectations. It will be recalled from Chapter 2 that one determinant of self-esteem is the discrepancy or gap between what a child *hopes* to become and where he currently sees himself. If the discrepancy is great, self-esteem is low; if the discrepancy is small – or becoming smaller – self-esteem is likely to be enhanced. We see here the link with expectations. If expectations are set *too* high, they become a threat to self-esteem. On the other hand, if we reduce expectations too much, there will be little or no progress, and so feelings of competence will not be developed. Albert Bandura, the originator of the theory of self-efficacy (see Bandura, 1992), pointed out that if people experience only easy successes their confidence is unlikely to develop since they come to expect quick results and are then easily discouraged by failure. So, getting the balance right is important. The comments earlier (and in the previous chapter) about teachers using their knowledge to match work to children's ability should go some way to ensuring effective challenges. However, there is one other potential problem.

Children can set *themselves* unrealistic goals; there is value in teachers being sensitive to this and, if necessary, speaking to parents about this. To illustrate the point: a phenomenon experienced by many primary teachers is one of boys who have set their hearts on being footballers, but who are not talented in this respect. Bearing in mind the theories mentioned in the previous paragraph, there is a real danger to self-esteem in cases where the gap between what children aspire to achieve and what they are actually capable of achieving is so wide. In such cases, although teachers will not want to shatter the idealistic dreams of children, they may be able to help by sensitively suggesting more modest targets or alerting children to other possibilities.

Two obvious ways in which this can be done are to help the child to become more aware of other talents or interests that might be more productive or rewarding for the individual concerned, and by providing a range of opportunities for children to try. To stay with the example of our boy who dreams of being a football star, there might be value in providing a range of other sporting opportunities – taster sessions in different sports and hobbies in which he may achieve some success. In recent years, this has in fact become more common in primary schools. In addition to introducing children to new sports, such policies may also have benefits for some children in terms of self-esteem.

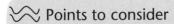 Points to consider

- What factors do you take into account when setting expectations of pupils?
- What are the difficulties associated with this process?
- How have you managed to overcome such difficulties?
- Can you identify any children in your class who might have expectations which are *too* high? What can be done about this?

Chapter summary and conclusion

The last two chapters have identified and discussed a number of strategies that we as teachers can use to help develop a sense of self-competence in the pupils we teach. The previous chapter focused on specific techniques which can be employed in the classroom. This chapter looked at the mindsets which are consistent with enhancing competence, and what we can do to influence these. That sense of being a competent learner is not a sentiment that all children hold but the good news for children, and for us as teachers, is that we can do something about it. By encouraging positive beliefs about intelligence and effort, by using praise in a selective and honest way, by learning more about children's views on motivation and by setting high but realistic expectations, we can go a long way to enabling children to have a positive view of their own ability and the learning process. That positive but realistic view should help them to take control of their learning experiences and enhance beliefs about competence.

In the next chapter, we move on to look at the other dimension of self-esteem, and examine how teachers can enhance feelings of self-worth.

Some important tips

Do	Don't
• Vary groupings where possible	• Just stick with the same set grouping for all areas of the curriculum
• Allow children to see that movement is possible between groups in your classroom	• Simply use the groupings from the previous teacher
• Look for examples of negative beliefs about learning and try to counter these	• Let unhelpful beliefs about ability go unchallenged
• Encourage positive mindsets: intelligence is not fixed and children can become better if they work harder and smarter	• Underestimate the difference you can make by helping children to develop an internal locus of control and task orientations to learning
• Use techniques such as empathetic prefaces to support honest feedback	• Avoid telling children they have made a mistake
• Think carefully about the way you use praise	• Be fooled into thinking all praise is good
• Ensure that children know what they are being praised for; that is, use contingent praise	• Use over-generalised praise to enhance beliefs about competence
• Be aware that children react differently to praise	• Assume public praise is necessarily best, and that more is always better
• Ensure that praise is sincere and proportionate	• Take the risk that children will perceive your comments as insincere
• Praise with care!	• Praise indiscriminately
• Consider the extrinsic and intrinsic motivation you encourage in your classroom	• Depend only on currently fashionable reward systems
• Learn more about the motivational drivers of your pupils: the range of motives they may have for working at a task	• See motivation only as intrinsic or based on tangible rewards
• Use knowledge about motivational mindsets to approach motivation from different perspectives at different times	• Believe that any one approach to motivation will cover all eventualities
• Beware the danger of an over-emphasis on rewards if children have gone beyond that stage and are appreciating the value of their learning	• Ignore a developmental trajectory for motivation as children move towards greater self-regulation

Do	Don't
• Have high but realistic expectations of behaviour and work	• Be inconsistent with your expectations
• Realise that by setting high expectations you are encouraging performance; it is this that enhances self-competence	• Assume that you are protecting children's self-esteem by not expecting too much
• Use a variety of techniques to reinforce the idea that 'we like to do our best at all times'	• Underestimate the messages that you give about standards by your own behaviour
• See mistakes and failures as good learning opportunities	• Avoid failure at all times because it is a threat to self-esteem
• Live this! *Demonstrate* how mistakes can be used to improve learning	• Convey messages that link failure to shame or embarrassment
• Use knowledge of the whole child to provide support to help meet high expectations	• Underestimate what children can achieve with your help
• Be alert to any children who may have unrealistically high expectations	• Ignore unrealistic expectations

Further reading

1. For more on the work of Carol Dweck, see:
- Dweck, C.S. (1999) *Self-theories: Their Role in Motivation, Personality and Development.* Philadelphia, PA: Psychology Press.
- Dweck, C.S. (2007) *Mindset: The New Psychology of Success.* New York: Ballantine Books.

2. For more about the use and misuse of praise, see:
- Kohn, A. (1996) *Beyond Discipline: From Compliance to Community.* Alexandria, VA: ASCD.
- Smith, I. (1999) *Is Praise Always a Good Thing?* Dundee: SCCC.

3. For more on children and motivation, see:
- McLean, A. (2003) *The Motivated School.* London: Paul Chapman.
- Pressley, M., Dolezal, S.E., Raphael, L.M., Mohan, L., Roehrig, A.D. and Bogner, K. (2003) *Motivating Primary-Grade Students.* New York: The Guilford Press.
- Ryan, R.M. & Deci, E.L. (2000) Self-determination theory and the facilitation of intrinsic motivation, self development, and well-being. *American Psychologist*, 55 (1), 68–78.

4. For more on expectations, and other messages for pupils, see:
- Fox, R. (2005) *Teaching and Learning: Lessons from Psychology.* Oxford: Blackwell.
- Rosenthal, R. & Jacobson, L. (1968) *Pygmalion in the Classroom: Teachers' Expectations and Pupils' Intellectual Development.* New York: Holt, Rinehart and Winston.

7

Affirming Intrinsic Worth as an Individual

Key ideas in this chapter

In this chapter, we move on from thinking about self-competence to consider the strategies that can be used to enhance children's sense of self-worth. The focus is now on how children feel they are valued for the people they are – not for what they can do, or achieve in relation to schoolwork. As with the competence element, there are some strategies that can make a difference to individuals and their perception of self-worth. It is helpful to think of two strands to this. First, we have the idea of affirming the child's intrinsic value as an individual; this can be linked to the work of Carl Rogers (1961) on unconditional positive regard. Second, we can look at the way that children conduct themselves; stated simply, acting in a decent and caring way gives us good reason to feel better about ourselves. It follows that if we can encourage positive behaviour patterns in children, we might realistically expect benefits in their feelings of worth. Clearly, the role of teachers is important here in providing honest but supportive feedback about such conduct.

In this chapter, we start by looking at the first of these, affirming the child's intrinsic worth, and consider the following strategies:

(Continues)

(Continued)
- **strategy 1: the importance of teacher modelling**
- **strategy 2: pupil voice and decision making**
- **strategy 3: pupil concerns – investigating personally important issues**
- **strategy 4: using circle time as a vehicle for worth enhancement**
- **strategy 5: creating and maintaining a worth-based ethos.**

Introduction

Central to the two-dimensional model of self-esteem is the belief that self-competence and self-worth involve different sets of beliefs and appraisals. In the last two chapters, we looked at a number of strategies which have the potential to enhance feelings of self-competence in the children. In the current chapter, and that which follows, the focus shifts to beliefs about self-worth. For some teachers, this is seen as a more difficult goal, but this need not be the case. The strategies we suggest below point to ways in which we can make the most of the opportunities which arise naturally in daily classroom life to affirm children, to strengthen and build their sense of value – both as individuals and as members of the class, contributing to a positive, happy school community.

We established in an earlier chapter that a child's sense of worth essentially involves an appraisal that he or she has intrinsic value as an individual, irrespective of perceived ability. It involves feelings of acceptance, respect and affection. A person will experience feelings of worth if she believes she is accepted as a member of the group, is respected as an individual entitled to the same rights as everyone else, can count on support when needed, and is cared for by those she depends upon. Such beliefs are influenced greatly by the messages children pick up from significant adults (including, importantly, their teacher) and from their peers. How these people appear to view the individual, how they behave towards that person, the extent to which they include them in group activities, and how they appear to care about their hopes and their feelings – all of these influence judgements of worth.

But, there is an important element at work here. In addition to feelings of acceptance, self-worth is influenced by whether individuals believe they are leading a good life: 'doing the right thing' or behaving in a virtuous way. So, there is an element of 'right and wrong' here – a moral dimension – most clearly reflected in conduct. In such judgements, both the perceived views of others and self-appraisals are involved – and experienced teachers will know that the relative balance of these components varies depending on the age of the individual. However, the influence of conduct forms the basis of the following chapter. Here we look at ways to protect and nurture a child's belief about their intrinsic worth as an individual in a caring society.

Strategy 1: the importance of teacher modelling

A number of years ago, there was a very popular poster which appeared in many classrooms, doctors' surgeries and indeed homes; it was entitled 'Children Learn What they Live' and was based on the poem by Dorothy Law Nolte (Nolte, 1998). For those interested in developing the self-esteem of pupils, there appeared to be a great deal of common sense in the sentiments. The poem was a list of phrases such as, 'If children live with acceptance they learn how to love'; 'if children live with praise they learn to appreciate'; 'if children live with kindness and consideration they learn respect'; and so on. The underlying theme of the poem was simply that if parents and teachers are good role models, children can learn a great deal. No formal teaching needs to take place; the informal observation and experience of any kind of behaviour being modelled will have an impact on the child's learning for good or ill.

Having read this far, readers will realise that the issues in Law Nolte's poem relate specifically to the self-worth element of self-esteem. The poem also listed some negative behaviours which could have a deep and lasting negative impact on the child, and the poster served both as a stark warning and an encouragement for teachers and parents. A closer reading of the poem should alert us to the fact that it is not just the modelling of behaviour which is important in relation to the experiences highlighted; it is also the environment in which the child grows up that has the potential for good or ill. Much of the content of Chapters 7 and 8 focuses on the environment (specifically, the classroom) but clearly the teacher has a fundamental role to play here. Accordingly, this chapter starts and ends with the role of the teacher. We start by considering the teacher as a role model in the context of self-worth.

It will be recalled from Chapter 2 that the process of modelling involves individuals learning from the actions, responses and apparent beliefs of another person – in our case, the teacher. In essence, we are suggesting that if the teacher displays a healthy sense of self-worth, we would expect the children to benefit from this. The behaviours she demonstrates, the values she shares and the attitudes she appears to hold will inevitably influence how pupils think about themselves. We looked at this in Chapter 6 as part of an emphasis on competence, but it is equally important with worth. As teachers, if we accept the importance of such basic values as honesty, compassion and respect – and wish the children to appreciate these – we have to demonstrate such values on a daily basis. Through our dealings with children (and others who visit the classroom), we have to *live* such values in practice, and where possible make explicit links for children. Let us look at just a few issues here which relate to how such values can be communicated in the classroom.

How the teacher appears to view the individual is of central importance. If she asserts values of fairness and equality, and appears to treat everyone as being equally important, equally entitled to her time and attention, and of equal concern to her, then children may begin to identify with these characteristics. We have reason to believe they will internalise such beliefs and – hopefully – embrace similar values and adopt similar behaviours. This can then become a mutually reinforcing cycle in the community of the classroom. At the very least, children will receive the message that we are all of equal worth, irrespective of which group we are in, or how difficult we find classroom life at times. (Importantly, from the child's perspective, if I sign up to this belief, it has to apply not just to me but to everyone else; with rights come responsibilities. This is revisited in Chapter 8.)

Conveying such messages becomes easier for us as teachers if we adopt a holistic view of children. While we would still wish to recognise those children who do well academically, we must also look beyond the qualities we have traditionally valued in class: ability, diligence and neatness. Values such as honesty, compassion and responsibility are some which we would hope to recognise and reward in children. From the teacher's point of view, exemplifying such values is part of the modelling process; acknowledging them in others is equally important.

Of course, how the teacher values individuals is reflected in how she behaves towards them. There are several factors here, and these actually overlap with effective behaviour management. An important idea is one of being consistent in managing behaviour and interacting with children. As we have already established, the teacher has to be seen as valuing everyone equally – not favouring some children while being over-critical or dismissive of others who present more of a challenge. For many of us – not just children – differential treatment implies different worth. Balancing a range of factors when managing behaviour can present difficulties for teachers, and experienced practitioners have learned that valuing everyone equally is not quite the same as treating everyone in the same way. We return to aspects of behaviour management in the next chapter.

The extent to which teachers appear to care about the hopes and feelings of their pupils is important. Knowing the children – their lives outside school, their families and their interests – is a good starting point. Importantly, letting the children know you are aware of, and interested in, the bigger picture of their lives gives a message that they are worthy of their teacher's attention. Letting your pupils know that you are concerned for them as individuals (not just as learners in the classroom), that you are interested in what they choose to do, that you share their joys but empathise with their difficulties and disappointments – all of these messages indicate that they are people of some worth. Quite obviously, for some children this may be little more than they expect; but for others, deprived of interest or concern in other contexts, such messages may carry greater value than we might imagine.

Although many of these signs of interest can be conveyed on an individual basis through brief chats and comments in passing, it is a good idea to think about making time for such communications in the course of the busy school week. These themes can also be incorporated into classroom activities, most notably in personal, social and emotional (PSE) activities, where exploring issues of interest and concern to children further reinforces messages that we are interested in each other. We look more at this in strategy 3, below.

Respecting self and others is one aspect of modelling which teachers can really help pupils to address. The teacher is given so many opportunities in the course of the day to show pupils how to respect themselves and others and teachers do not have to have these listed. The very simple act of saying 'please' and 'thank you' shows that the person is worthy of being treated in a respectful way. Ensuring that the experience is the same for all is important; children will not only watch the teacher's interaction with other pupils in the class but also with the adults who visit the classroom.

Having said this, it is also worth remembering that we are working with children and we need to be careful that our expectations are realistic. Doing good things and making good choices is not always easy, either for children or adults. When a great deal of effort has been put into modelling and developing children's skills in making good choices, and then an incident occurs in the playground where it is clear that the whole class has ignored the lesson and their role model, it is easy to feel disappointed, to feel as if the strategy is not working. Perhaps this very incident can be used as an example of the consequences of a bad choice on themselves and others. Using real-life experiences and consequences of pupils' choices, good or bad, is an excellent opportunity to have a meaningful discussion; it can be time-consuming, but may be time well spent.

Finally here, sometimes it is necessary – or at least beneficial – to temper our messages. The real challenge is to be honest, particularly with children, in a gentle way; indeed this shows the pupils genuine respect and can protect their feelings of self-worth. It is interesting that when working with student teachers in identifying values that they would wish to promote when they have their own classroom, honesty and respect for self and others are almost always the two highlighted as most important. Despite their relative inexperience in the classroom, students recognise that although this will be a challenging task it is a most worthwhile aim.

 Activity 1

It has been suggested above that teachers can enhance self-worth if they give the message that everyone is equally important, equally entitled to time and attention, and of equal concern.

- Can you identify ways in which you do this?
- Can you identify some other potential ways in which the messages might be emphasised?

Thinking about values and attitudes:

- What values and attitudes do you hold dear?
- How important are such values and attitudes in children?
- How might you model these?

Strategy 2: pupil voice and decision making

This strategy is also related to the idea of affirmation. Again, the simple message here is that each child should feel valued as an individual – irrespective of their ability. Individuals can lack the skills and knowledge that their peers possess; they may also feel less attractive, have fewer possessions and be less popular with the peer group. None of these things should signify reduced worth as a human being. The question then arises, how can a teacher help children to feel valued in their own right?

One of the strategies a teacher can use is to let the children know, through the way she interacts with them and the way in which she manages day-to-day classroom life, that she values their opinions. Increasingly within the education context, we hear the phrase 'pupil voice'. This is certainly an important aspect of the *Curriculum for Excellence* agenda in Scotland and is also promoted across other parts of the UK. What is meant by this and how can we as teachers use this strategy to develop a pupil's sense of self-worth?

Pupil voice is often discussed in relation to citizenship activities in schools. The citizenship idea of democracy and rights and responsibilities (revisited in Chapter 8) encourages pupils in schools to have their say and to be part of the decision-making process which will address issues directly affecting their learning, their school life and indeed their future. There are good reasons for this approach from a self-worth perspective, although it is likely that many teachers may value such activities for other reasons as well.

One of those other reasons is that when pupils are involved in the decision-making process they have a vested interest in the success of the venture. Take, for example, classroom rules; when these are decided in collaboration with the children, the process will involve a level of discussion about why a particular rule is important to the pupils and to the smooth running of the classroom. Children will all have an opportunity to say what they think is important to them in relation to the classroom environment. When they then see these rules displayed in the classroom, they will have a sense of ownership and a much greater understanding of their relevance. In the case of rules, we hope that one consequence is that the children are more likely to comply with them. We revisit this issue in the following chapter.

But there are many other opportunities to show children that their opinions are valued. Events such as organising school trips or sports days, arranging coffee mornings for the elderly in the local community or storytelling for early years classes are all relatively common in primary schools. The children can be involved in the decision-making process and can see in practice that the knowledge, opinions and ideas that they have shared in class have been taken seriously.

From our, more specific, self-worth perspective, how does engaging the pupils in the type of activities above help to develop a sense of self-worth in the pupil? Well, unless the teacher is aware of the possibility that this can be achieved through these kinds of activities, then it may not help in this; however, if she is aware and is committed to developing a sense of self-worth, then this can be a very positive experience for pupils. Stated simply, by listening to pupils' suggestions, we give a strong message that their opinions matter and are worthy of consideration. They are accepted as valued members of the class community. Sharing ideas and opinions can be much more linked to personality than to ability, and pupils who may not be strong academically are sometimes just as able to offer suggestions in relation to ideas or organisation. When they see these ideas coming to fruition, they can then feel a sense of value. They appreciate that the teacher has listened to what they have to say and that this is important and can make a huge difference as to how pupils view each other and themselves.

More and more, we are seeing an extension of decision-making opportunities, from organisational aspects of classroom life to learning processes. In many classrooms, children are being encouraged to be part of the decision making about what it is they want to learn and how they might be taught. This perhaps works best in areas such as topic work and so on. Indeed, many of our early years colleagues have been engaging in this kind of activity for years. We would argue that, providing this activity does not disadvantage the progress in children's learning, there are certainly benefits to be gained in the involvement of the children. A word of caution, however – if you engage in this kind of activity, then you must be prepared to go along with at least some of the suggestions and ideas of the pupils. If none of their ideas ever turn into reality, they will very quickly assume that their voice and opinions do not really matter, that the teacher is not genuinely listening to the voice of the class. In self-esteem terms, this would have a negative, not a positive, effect on beliefs about worth.

Finally, this requires a degree of flexibility on the part of the teacher. As an illustration, a colleague once decided to allow pupils to vote on the topic of the class assembly, feeling quite sure she would be able to 'sway' the pupils to her choice. In a very public vote, her choice of Remembrance Day fitting very nicely into the class project was overwhelmingly voted out by the class for an assembly to demonstrate their new skills in speaking French!

Activity 2

Think of your classroom over the course of a week:

- What kind of decisions are the children involved in making?
- Which of these are organisational and which are linked to learning?
- Are all children involved in these discussions?
- Can you think of pupils who do not appear to engage in the decision-making process?
- If so, how could you encourage them to participate?

Strategy 3: pupil concerns – investigating personally important issues

Clearly, this follows on from the points above about encouraging pupil voice. Two educational purposes (at least) are served when children engage in learning about issues of interest to them – one which is general in nature and one which relates specifically to self-esteem. The more general purpose concerns benefits in terms of intrinsic motivation and authentic learning. We know that when children see work as being relevant to them, they are more likely to engage with it. The second, more specific, purpose is to convey a message to children that their own interests and feelings – and by extension, they themselves – are valued.

It has been suggested that there is a set of 'foundation conditions' necessary for encouraging pupil voice (Rudduck, 2003). These are: a climate in the classroom or school that is marked by trust and openness; accepting pupils as individuals with genuine interest in discussing classroom activity – and the ability to do so in a meaningful way; and valuing 'life skills' alongside academic achievement. It seems clear to us that these conditions link very clearly with the range of processes we have discussed above in relation to self-worth.

We have already mentioned some of the ways in which children can be involved in choices about the work they are engaged in. We look here at just one aspect of this: activities related to personal, social and emotional development. Advice on such activities is included in many texts and curricular documents available to schools. The terminology tends to change from time to time, but many fundamental issues remain relatively constant. At the risk of oversimplification, most PSE programmes and publications share the aim of helping children to understand themselves and others, and to learn skills of interacting with peers in the belief that these will help them to develop as confident and competent social beings. Typical areas for discussion include the following:

- Expressing my feelings
- Being a member of a group
- Things that are important to me
- Listening to other people
- Helping others
- How my behaviour affects those around me
- Making hard choices
- Feeling good about myself
- Working well with others
- Understanding other people's views
- Solving problems with my friends

This is simply an illustrative list and, for many teachers, these or similar topics will be addressed in the course of a term, often through discussions or circle time sessions. From a self-worth perspective, a message worth conveying is that these issues – of concern to most children at some point – are included as a direct consequence of the fact that they are relevant to them. In addition, the teacher who is aware of how feelings of self-worth are influenced can monitor the content and reinforce and mediate important messages.

For those readers keen to develop this aspect of practice, the 'Social and Emotional Aspects of Learning' (SEAL) programme which is endorsed by the UK Department of Education, is one example of a PSE programme which has proved to be effective. It focuses on the areas of self-awareness, self-regulation, motivation, empathy and social skills. The approach is based on the work of Daniel Goleman (1995) on emotional intelligence. The programme targets a range of attitudes, beliefs, skills and behaviours related to the five areas above. While having a distinctive theoretical framework, the SEAL programme shares features with many other PSE programmes (Humphrey et al., 2008).

> ### ▦ Activity 3
>
> Looking at the sample list of PSE topics above, and adding any of your own:
>
> - Which topics have you found to be successful for activities or discussions? Why was this?
> - Which have been less successful? Again, why do you think this was?
> - To what extent were you conscious of helping to mediate or moderate the messages being explored at that time?
> - Reflecting back, can you think of any changes you might make to any of these activities to reinforce messages related to self-worth?

Strategy 4: using circle time as a vehicle for worth enhancement

In the past two decades, for many schools in the UK (and beyond), the practice of circle time has been promoted as a way to enhance the self-esteem of children. In many respects, it seems to have become the default 'self-esteem programme' in primary school settings. The fact that it has gained such popularity would seem to indicate that teachers have found it to be effective, but the research evidence to support such a belief has proven somewhat elusive. There is not space here to examine such evidence in detail, but the interested reader is referred to the paper by Miller and Moran (2007) referred to at the end of this chapter for more information about its origins and the research evidence. The good news for advocates of circle time is that the same paper demonstrates that the approach *can* influence feelings of self-worth.

As we outlined in Chapter 4, that study looked at two different approaches to self-esteem enhancement to see whether there was any effect on measured self-esteem. Three groups of teachers were involved: one group regularly used the circle time approach, one group used methods to encourage beliefs about efficacy (i.e. self-competence) and the third acted as a control group. In all, 21 teachers and their classes were involved. The period of investigation was four months, and measures of self-esteem were taken at the start and the end of the period. The findings indicated that both approaches contributed to improvements in self-esteem – but the important thing was that the two approaches achieved their results in different ways. Whereas the efficacy-based approach, focusing on the achievement of performance goals, worked through the self-competence dimension, circle time worked by enhancing feelings of self-worth.

So, given that there is now some evidence to show that circle time can improve feelings of self-worth, teachers can feel reassured that alongside the enjoyment that most pupils appear to get from the weekly circle time session, one aspect of self-esteem may be developed and nurtured. But clearly this will depend on how the teacher uses the technique. So, what do we know about how best to implement it in practice? The first thing that has to be said is that there is no shortage of practitioner-focused books on the technique, and so we provide only the briefest of outlines here (for more information, see Gutteridge and Smith, 2005; Mosley, 1996, 1998).

In the UK, the version of circle time most frequently used in schools owes much to the work of Jenny Mosley. Although there are other producers of circle time texts and teaching resources, Mosley's approach seems to be the most comprehensive and her methodology the most clearly developed, with the techniques having evolved steadily since her early work in *Turn Your School Round* (1993). The ideas are very accessible and the books give a number of examples and reasons why the activities would be valuable for children. Many in the field of education also like the way Mosley encourages teachers to take care of themselves, identifying the challenging role of teacher and the stresses it often brings. For these teachers, the demonstration of Mosley's understanding of their chosen career gave her, and therefore her approach and suggested programme, a real credibility.

For many local authorities, the approach was seen as a panacea to playground problems, particularly bullying. Alongside the book, Mosley could be brought in to deliver professional development days for staff. In these sessions, she would talk a group of teachers through the approach. Often children from a local school would be invited and Mosley would successfully model the approach, often with pupils who had no experience of circle time. Her enthusiasm and obvious commitment to the approach, and the enjoyment of the children, was often effective in convincing local authorities and teachers to buy into this idea. We are not in a position to comment on the bigger picture of circle time approaches and their effect on the whole-school community; we leave readers to form their own judgements of the ambitious claims made for such work. We focus instead on a very simple question: why might circle time influence feelings of self-worth?

When children take part in a circle time activity, there are organisational and procedural factors which have symbolic significance, emphasising key messages about the worth of the individual. The circular format, with children – and adults – seated either on the floor or on chairs, emphasises equality of status. The rules about each person speaking in turn, while others listen politely, emphasise the idea that everyone is entitled to express their views. (Interestingly, such rules also point to a responsibility to listen to the views expressed by the other members of the circle.) The fact that children are often involved in choosing the topics gives a message about their thoughts and feelings being of importance. The responses of a sensitive teacher, who acknowledges children's feelings, concerns and hopes, can further support the belief that individuals have intrinsic worth, irrespective of their status in other aspects of classroom life. In short, circle time can provide a context in which individuals feel respected and valued; it is this feature which is likely to help children to develop a sense of self-worth.

Of course, as with any classroom processes, the role of the teacher is of central importance. So, what factors would we suggest that teachers bear in mind when using circle time as a means of enhancing self-worth? Perhaps the single most important piece of advice is to be aware of the factors which influence feelings of self-worth (as discussed in this chapter and the one that follows). Think about the processes related to affirmation mentioned above, and those related to proactive behaviour and other aspects of conduct which we discuss in Chapter 8. If you are aware of these factors, then you will be on the alert for interactions and messages which can have an effect on children in the circle. In addition:

• Think carefully about the topics; plan them carefully, and for a reason.
  ○ Consider themes you wish to develop – for example, ways in which we can help others
  ○ Look at issues which may have arisen in the class or playground that you wish to explore with the children
  ○ Ensure that the children's ideas or topics are included wherever possible
• As you contribute to the session, be aware of the messages that are being conveyed in the circle and their potential for influencing self-worth. You may wish to add a contribution which amplifies or modifies a previous statement if you see a significant worth-based issue emerging.
• Think about the organisational factors:
  ○ The location – away from doors, corridors and other distractions
  ○ Comfort – the length of sessions will vary with the age of the children,

but with older classes, where they may extend a bit longer, the participants need to be comfortable
- ○ Timing: it is not something that we regularly 'shoe-horn' in at the end of the day (or week); how often would we do that with maths or language?
- Try to ensure you create the correct balance in terms of a positive tone (and status):
  - ○ Give the message that circle time is not just a time-filler; it is as important as other 'work'
  - ○ ... but it should not be seen as a chore!
  - ○ Incorporate some fun elements (unless this would be inappropriate, given the topic)
  - ○ Emphasise that circle time can help us all, individually and as a class
  - ○ Be aware of your own messages: demonstrate enthusiasm
- Act as just another member of the circle where possible.
  - ○ Be mindful of modelling and reinforcing appropriate responses
  - ○ Show enthusiasm and gratitude for all contributions
  - ○ Avoid asserting authority in the circle unless absolutely necessary
- Be aware of other strategies to employ if sensitive issues arise or children wish to discuss more personal matters (such as 'Bubble Time' or 'Think Books').

▦ Activity 4

If circle time is an activity you use frequently in your classroom, consider the last few sessions which have taken place.

- What topics have been discussed?
- To what extent have these been specially selected for the purpose?
- Have children been exposed to honest feedback from their peers?
- To what extent have you tried to mediate messages?
- Think of some of your own responses within the circle; can children use you as a model for developing the skills of giving an honest and appropriate response?

If you do not normally employ circle time:

- Can you outline the reasons why?
- In the light of your understanding of the factors which influence self-worth, do you think it could be adapted to suit your purpose? If so, how?
- If you remain unconvinced by circle time, can you think of other contexts or vehicles for the enhancement of self-worth?

Strategy 5: creating and maintaining a worth-based ethos

So far, we have suggested several ways in which we can help to enhance feelings of worth in children. We have looked at issues related to the teacher as a role model, at pupil voice, and ways of involving children more in educational decision making, and at how circle time can help us. We now consider how a nurturing, worth-based ethos can provide the backdrop for the strategies and techniques employed in the class.

It can be a very difficult task to try and explain the school ethos to student teachers, even to those who may not long be out of the school system themselves. The ethos can be thought of as the normal 'character' or 'tone' of a school – or even its 'spirit'; but capturing the essence of a positive ethos is not straightforward. For many, a positive school ethos is seen as being a little like the wind; we know when it is there and we know when it is not, but we do not always know the cause or the reason for its presence or absence. Certainly, it is more than a bright environment or a warm welcome or happy faces; although these are all important, it goes deeper than that, right to the values and the heart of the community.

In many respects, the ethos of the school is reflected in the shared practices and the shared beliefs – some explicit, some implicit – about what is important in the school and its community. We can make a distinction between the official statements of ethos which appear in documentation (the values and beliefs which the school officially endorses) and what is actually experienced by those who work in the school. Often, the former make reference to issues such as policy on school uniform and homework and acts of collective worship. While these may indeed contribute in some way to ethos, our interest relates more to the ongoing personal, social and learning messages which constitute children's experience of school. In fact, we believe that the focus of this book is consistent with such a perspective; if we understand how the ongoing experiences of school life can impact upon children's sense of worth, we can make the most of the opportunities that occur.

Ethos indicators introduced in both Scottish and English education systems in the late 1990s included 12 distinct criteria, including the morale of both pupils and teachers, the nature of the learning context, the quality of teacher–pupil relationships and equality and justice. Looking at these for a moment, and reflecting on what we have considered on our journey so far, we can see how the morale of pupils is influenced by the extent to which they feel they are achieving success (beliefs about competence) and are valued as individuals (feelings of worth). Similar comments apply equally to teachers, of course! We can also see how the nature of the learning context is influential in children's appraisals of worth – not least in the extent to which they feel that they and their views are valued. Similarly, as the reader will undoubtedly have realised already, the quality of teacher–pupil relationships is central to children's perceptions of self-worth. Finally, issues related to fairness and justice are discussed in Chapter 8, when we consider exploring values through the curriculum. It seems almost unnecessary to have to point out that both worth and competence are inextricably linked to ethos.

In fact, most experienced teachers do not have to be convinced of the value to pupils, both in relation to their learning and to their sense of self-worth, of a positive school ethos. It is certainly the case that the importance of strong, effective and positive leadership has recently been recognised as playing an important role in the success of schools, and a great deal of discussion has taken place at local and national level on how to support and develop this in teachers and head teachers. Through staff meetings, pupil council meetings and parent associations or boards, the head teacher needs to lead by example, share the vision and enthuse all involved. A sense of ownership for the whole community is really important to success. Children will respond best when they are clear about the expectations of the school and its entire staff. (This point can be related to the discussion in Chapter 8 about the key characteristics of behaviour management policies in relation to self-worth.) The learning community should feel that they have the responsibility and the power to make a difference: 'this is our school and we are all in it together'.

Outward signs of a worth-based positive ethos can be simple and obvious. In addition to many of the issues we have discussed in previous chapters, a school team that demonstrates a polite and courteous approach to adults and children will be clearly modelling respect for all. The importance of being a positive role model has already been discussed and this is certainly an example of when it can work well. Saying 'please' and 'thank you', holding doors open and so on may seem fairly trivial, but these small things set standards and they are things that even the very youngest pupils can pick up on. Often these are the first examples of a positive ethos a visitor gets when entering the school; it is noticeable and it does impress.

Bright displays throughout the school celebrating the lives and the work of pupils also convey messages about what is valued in the school. In the foyer of many school buildings, there is an achievement wall or book, a display cabinet or shelves – something which allows the visitor to see how children and their success can be recognised. A school which is attuned to self-worth would ensure that the 'successes' being celebrated include those involving *character* as well as competence – for example, charitable acts and contributions to the community, in addition to the more usual sporting and academic successes. These displays are an outward-facing sign of what is important in a school community and certainly give those visiting the school a sense of the values and purposes that the community hold dear. For the children, they serve as a reminder of the esteem in which they are held; they are ways of amplifying messages about worth and competence. Such public displays of achievement and attainment say very clearly 'this school is proud of you'.

Obviously, in relation to learning, a positive school ethos is equally important; instilling in children a 'can do' attitude can be a real challenge on the part of the teacher. This has been central to discussion in Chapters 5 and 6, and there is no need to revisit the issues here. A word of caution though; a 'can do' attitude does not and should not mean that all children are capable of all things. Indeed, it will be recalled from discussion in previous chapters that such beliefs – essentially that all children are winners, capable of achieving whatever they want – are amongst the questionable beliefs from which we would wish to distance ourselves. It seems self-evident that all children 'can do' a variety of things but no one 'can do' everything. More realistically, if we wish to convey messages that children are valued as learners, we should think about the extent to which all children are included in classroom life, the way activities are organised to encourage cooperation and mutual support, the way we incorporate pupil voice, and the extent to which pupils can approach teachers with confidence that they will receive a sympathetic audience. In short, we are talking about messages about equity, concern and fairness. These should be central to an ethos which values self-worth.

When teachers are working in a positive environment, they too can feel the benefits. They are not working in isolation; they are working towards a common goal, hopefully one which they have been instrumental in shaping. If children are constantly being exposed to affirming and optimistic responses, not only for their learning and by the class teacher but in all aspects of their school life, then their chances of becoming effective contributors to their community are much higher.

To conclude this section, as we suggested earlier, the creation of a positive worth-enhancing ethos goes beyond the limited selection of issues discussed here. At the very least, it can be seen as a combination of the techniques and beliefs in all five strategies in this chapter – together with those which will be discussed in the next chapter. All of these – and more – are relevant to how a range of practices and beliefs about individuals, schools and society come together to form the ethos in a classroom and school.

∿ Points to consider

Sometimes it is difficult to appreciate the ethos of your own school or classroom, particularly if you have been there for a period of time, or alternatively, if it is your first appointment. Try to arrange a visit to another school to learn more about its ethos.

- To what extent do you feel there is a difference? What signs alert you to this?
- What signals are you picking up about beliefs and practices in relation to:
  - Learning?
  - Relationships?
  - Responsibilities?
  - Routines?
- Do you feel there are other factors which influence the 'feel' of the school? If so, what might these be?

Chapter summary and conclusion

In this chapter, we have turned our attention to the self-worth element of self-esteem and how this can be promoted and developed in the classroom. It will be noted that none of the previously popular 'special' activities or instant remedies appear here. Instead we have looked at day-to-day life in a primary classroom from a self-worth perspective. The good news is that a great deal of what class teachers already undertake on a daily basis can indeed help to promote self-worth in pupils. What may have been missing in the past is the underpinning theory of why teachers are doing what we are doing. There may be activities discussed in this chapter that teachers had not previously linked to the development of self-worth; a deeper understanding of the benefits children can acquire from such opportunities should encourage teachers to consider making more of these.

Finally, there is an important point to be emphasised here: none of the techniques or strategies we have discussed *guarantees* the enhancement of self-worth. It is not the techniques themselves that are the key factor; the teacher is the catalyst. More specifically, it is her *psychological and pedagogical knowledge* that holds the key. The teacher needs to (a) understand how self-worth is influenced, and (b) *see the potential* in these activities from a worth-based perspective. From this she can create meaningful worth-enhancing messages and experiences.

In the next chapter, we maintain our focus on self-worth, but look in particular at its relationship with conduct.

Some important tips

Do	Don't
• Be aware of your influence as a role model	• Underestimate how much children learn from watching you – even when you are not aware of it
• Be explicit about values of fairness, equality and compassion and how these can work in practice	• Assume that children will make links between such values and their own behaviours
• Work to demonstrate desirable values through your own interactions with the children and others	• Underestimate the extent to which your own actions will amplify the messages you give
• Let children see they are all of equal importance to you	• Give children reasons to believe you value some individuals more than others
• Get to know the bigger picture of the children's lives	• Focus only on schoolwork and academic attainment
• Make time to discuss children's interests, hopes and concerns	• See this as a waste of valuable teaching time
• Be aware of pupil voice: give children an opportunity to have their say on matters that concern them	• Ask for children's views when you know you won't or can't take them on board
• Show that you are listening and genuinely interested	• Address issues of pupil voice in a tokenistic way
• Enable children to take responsibility in the classroom	• Give opportunities for responsibility only to the more able or 'trustworthy' children
• Allow children to investigate personally relevant issues through PSE activities	• Limit PSHE activities to a set list of topics to be covered
• Think through the issues in advance of the lesson, and be aware of the potential for influencing self-worth	• Rely on your ability to react on an ad-hoc basis to children's comments
• Be prepared to engage (sensitively) with the children's views to mediate important messages	• Pass by opportunities to engage with issues related to self-worth

Do	Don't
• Consider the benefits of circle time as a forum for enhancing self-worth	• Assume that circle time will automatically enhance self-esteem
• Ensure that the process is followed carefully to emphasise each child's right to be heard	• Relax the rules, particularly about turn taking and listening respectfully to each other
• Spend time selecting topics for these sessions which have direct relevance to self-worth issues	• Miss the opportunity to discuss relevant issues of concern to pupils in a safe environment
• Let the children know that you value circle time and the opportunities to discuss issues of interest	• Use circle time as a time-filler or convey messages that you don't see it as important
• Be a good role model by responding in a caring but honest manner	• Feel you have to be positive in your responses at all times
• Be aware of a range of factors that can contribute to a positive ethos – messages about ongoing learning and relationships, responsibilities and routines	• Assume that ethos is determined primarily by whole-school policies on traditional issues such as uniform and homework
• Explain, and demonstrate through your own actions, the sort of behaviour and attitudes that contribute to a positive ethos	• Leave it to chance that these factors will be automatically understood by children in the class
• Take all opportunities to highlight for children how they can contribute to a warm and caring ethos	• Assume that it is only the adults who create the class and school ethos
• Always be on the look-out for processes which can carry messages about self-worth	• Focus only on the 'learning' aspects of classroom processes
• Appreciate that your psychological and pedagogical knowledge is a key component in enhancing beliefs about worth	• Believe that it is the activities or processes *in themselves* which will enhance self-worth

Further reading

1. For more on pupil voice, see:
- Cheminais, R. (2008) *Engaging Pupil Voice to Ensure that Every Child Matters: A Practical Guide*. London: David Fulton.
- Flutter, J. & Rudduck, J. (2004) *Consulting Pupils: What's in It for Schools?* London: RoutledgeFalmer.
- Rudduck, J. (2003) *Consulting Pupils about Teaching and Learning*. Teaching and Learning Research Briefing. Available at: www.tlrp.org/pub/documents/no5_ruddock.pdf

2. For more on personal, social and emotional aspects of education, see:
- Brown, M. (2009) *Personal, Social and Emotional Development*. Carlton: Curriculum Corporation.
- Dowling, M. (2009) *Young Children's Personal, Social and Emotional Development*. London: Sage.

- Humphrey, N., Kalambouka, A., Bolton, J., Lendrum, A., Wigelsworth, M., Lennie, C. & Farrell, P. (2008) *Primary Social and Emotional Aspects of Learning (SEAL) Evaluation of Small Group Work*. Nottingham: DCSF Publications.

3. For more on using circle time, see:

- Gutterige, D. & Smith, V. (2005) *Using Circle Time for PSHE and Citizenship: A Year's Plan for Key Stage 2 Teachers*. Oxford: David Fulton.
- Mosley, J. (1996) *Quality Circle Time in the Primary Classroom*. Cambridge: LDA.
- Mosley, J. (1998) *More Quality Circle Time*. Cambridge: LDA.

4. For a more critical examination of circle time, see:

- Miller, D.J. & Moran, T.R. (2007) Theory and practice in self-esteem enhancement: circle time and efficacy-based approaches – a controlled evaluation. *Teachers and Teaching: Theory and Practice*, 13 (6), 601–15

5. To read more about ethos, see:

- Nolte, D. (1998) *Children Learn What They Live: Parenting to Inspire Values*. New York: Workman Publishing.
- Smith, R. (2004) *Creating the Effective Primary School: A Guide for School Leaders and Teachers*. London: Routledge. (See Chapters 1 and 2.)

8

The Role of Conduct: Living According to Good Principles

Key ideas in this chapter

We continue here to look at how we can help individuals to develop a sense of self-worth, by looking at several issues related to conduct. Some of these concern the ways in which children can be encouraged to help others – what is known as *pro-social* behaviour. Others relate to general conduct, in the class and elsewhere, and the role of the teacher in providing support and guidance. It could be argued that Chapters 7 and 8 reflect two differing, but complementary, perspectives on self-worth enhancement. In Chapter 7, underpinning our discussion of the intrinsic worth of the individual was an implicit belief in terms of *entitlement;* a belief that all children are equally entitled to be accepted for who they are, and to be treated with care and respect. In contrast, Chapter 8 touches on *opportunities* and *responsibilities* in this area – opportunities for developing one's own sense of worth and responsibilities for nurturing the worth of others.

In order to do this, we look at the following:

- strategy 1: 'doing good' and required helpfulness
- strategy 2: the value of peer tutoring
- strategy 3: the role of behaviour codes
- strategy 4: looking to the curriculum for opportunities.

Introduction

In the previous chapter, we looked at a range of issues for teachers to bear in mind if they wish to enhance feelings of worth in their pupils; essentially these were about affirming the intrinsic worth of an individual. However, it will be recalled from earlier discussions that there is another strand to feelings of self-worth; this relates to the idea of virtue – the conviction that one is living out a good life, 'doing the right thing'. Although there are cultural differences in terms of those behaviours considered 'good' or worthy of respect, within most societies there exists a shared set of values and principles which contribute to the norms of society. In most cases, these include beliefs about honesty, compassion, consideration for others, truth, fairness, and so on. In practice, the values shared by a society form a reference point when considering what is – and what is not – good behaviour.

From an individual perspective, decisions about whether you are leading a good life are influenced by two sources: from the messages received from others about your conduct, and from your own self-appraisals. In keeping with the approach we have adopted throughout this book, we do not advocate artificially enhancing self-beliefs by misleading children and suggesting that they are being helpful or behaving well when they are not. Quite apart from the practical problems that this may create, and the ethical issues it raises, we have established at several points that genuine self-esteem is based on real behaviours and honest appraisals. Given this stance, therefore, how can we enhance self-worth by focusing on conduct?

In short, our focus is on ways to encourage and then recognise 'good' conduct, and in so doing, increase a sense of self-worth in individuals. This is likely to happen in two ways. First, when individuals choose to help others, or conduct themselves in a positive, supportive and socially approved manner, they are more likely to regard themselves in a favourable light. Second, by behaving in such a way, they are likely to gain messages of approval from others, thus further enhancing beliefs about their worth.

Strategy 1: 'doing good' and required helpfulness

For most people, there is a sense of personal satisfaction one gets from helping or assisting another. When children are being – and are praised for being – kind, caring and considerate to others, there is no doubt that this can contribute to a sense of self-worth. Importantly, it is not about what they can do, or how clever they may be, but about what kind of a person they are; and that really is at the heart of each and every human being. What can teachers do to encourage and reward such positive characteristics?

Research studies have shown that teachers tend to use praise more frequently for work than behaviour. We tend to see praise as an effective way to reward – and further encourage – the quality of work, the goals children achieve, and so on. The evidence suggests we are less likely to praise pupils for behaviour, perhaps because we feel we are entitled to *expect* good behaviour in our classes. Of course, behaviour is not just about following the rules; it includes children showing consideration or kindness to others, taking time to help peers with a problem in their work, or ensuring others are included in playground games or groups. Importantly, for the children on the receiving end of such a gesture, it could mean the difference between coming to school and not coming to school. Such caring actions often go unnoticed and unrecognised in many school situations – not surprisingly, since many of them may not happen in the classroom but in the corridor, in the playground or in the lunch hall. Children who intuitively or routinely do good things for other people often do so without any recognition, but highlighting or rewarding such behaviour can have a two-fold effect in the classroom.

First, for those pupils who are thoughtful and caring of others – most certainly characteristics we would see as desirable in friends – praising these traits and the associated acts is acknowledging the value of that person. Even putting aside for one moment our interest in self-worth, this seems only right and proper. It is interesting that children who are inclusive and caring of others are often recognised by and popular with their peers. In the class of a colleague, one such pupil had been off for a few days with a bad cold; on his return the class burst into a spontaneous round of applause! There was clear recognition on the part of the rest of the class that this pupil made a difference to the quality of their lives, and the colleague was quick to point out that she did not get the same response when she returned from an absence!

The second benefit to recognising and rewarding this kind of behaviour is in the example it sets to other pupils. It is not easy for some children to be kind and thoughtful; as we know, some adults do not manage this. Highlighting pupils for whom this comes more naturally can have a very positive effect on others in the class. It gives them examples, clues and ideas that they might be able to follow, leading them (we hope) to possibly act in a more caring way themselves. It provides examples at the child's own level which are likely to appear relevant and authentic to their peers. In this respect, 'catching them doing good' can be even more effective than creating situations in order to praise them for doing what we have directed them to do. But 'catching children doing good' is not always easy; teachers have to work hard at being observant, taking account of events both in and out of the classroom. It also requires a view of the teacher's role which goes beyond academic learning. Of course, other children and adults in the school can help by bringing situations to our attention and passing on information. But, as teachers, we can supplement these naturally occurring events with some others – while being conscious of making them authentic and worthwhile.

One technique that is often used in school, and which can help to foster feelings of self-worth, is pupils taking on responsibility for helping others. Many schools use this in fairly formal ways in learning situations and activities such as peer tutoring (which we discuss below) but other schemes which focus less on learning and more on social and personal factors, for example, 'buddy systems' or 'playground friends' schemes, are also very useful. Older children can experience a sense of responsibility – and enhanced worth – when they are looked up to by younger children or when they are asked to help, either by an adult or by the pupil's 'buddy' in a playground situation. For most pupils, this kind of commitment to others and the personal reward they can acquire from this interaction gives them an opportunity to be recognised for who they are and how they interact and care for others. It gives them a message that what they are doing is a good thing and that people like and appreciate them for doing that.

There are many opportunities for teachers to provide pupils with the opportunity to experience being valued for who they are. As a passing thought, is this not also the case for us as teachers? Is it not also true that feeling valued by others, colleagues or school management, also makes the teacher's job a great deal more fulfilling and enjoyable?

To return to the main theme of this section: the idea of giving children increased responsibility can be related to the idea of *required helpfulness*. This is a term borrowed from the literature on resilience (see Werner and Smith, 1992). Mainstream literature in that area identifies self-esteem as a protective factor – a personality characteristic which helps children to overcome negative life events. More recently, it has been argued that the two dimensions of self-esteem have a much closer relationship with resilience than had previously been acknowledged (see, for example, Miller and Daniel, 2007; Jindall-Snape and Miller, 2008). Certainly, children are more likely to come through experiences of trauma or adversity if they believe they are entitled to a happy, healthy life – and have some expectation of receiving care and respect. That is, self-worth is a protective factor in resilience.

According to Newman (2004), a 'positive school experience' which promotes a sense of self-efficacy is also an important factor in building resilience. It will be recalled from the theoretical discussions earlier in this book that self-efficacy and self-competence are effectively synonymous, and consequently many of the strategies focusing on competence in Chapters 5 and 6 are likely to help to build up children's resilience. However, our focus here is on feelings of worth, and in this respect, requiring children to help others has considerable potential. The point about required helpfulness is that children realise that others are *depending* upon them; they are helping someone who *needs* their assistance. In most societies and in most contexts, such behaviour is valued; individuals who are engaged in such work are 'doing good': showing caring or helpful or pro-social behaviour. It is in these associations that we see the influence on children's sense of worth.

By encouraging pupils to take on roles in the classroom which are seen to be assisting the teacher and other children, children feel 'helpful', trusted and valued. A fair and equal system of classroom organisation which identifies helpers who assist with tasks, give out books, collect resources and so on is common in most classrooms. For many children, such activities in isolation may not be hugely significant in the development of a sense of self-worth, but when they accumulate, and are linked to other worth-enhancing strategies, and reinforced by messages from the teacher about the value of such work to their community, the effect can be beneficial. Importantly, for those children who lack self-worth, such messages may have particular value.

Additionally, it should be noted that such small daily routines give children a sense of structure; this structure gives a security and a safe framework for pupils to grow, to learn and at times to make mistakes. This relates to the ethos of the classroom, discussed in the previous chapter. It can often be pupils' perceptions rather than anything the teacher has said that instils a sense of fear at the idea of failure. Yet it is very often only through failing and having the courage to try again and again that a real sense of achievement is reached. The teacher's role in such situations is to focus on the intent – that is, the desire to help – and to let the children know that this is appreciated.

It is not difficult for teachers to give children opportunities to help in the classroom environment – indeed it can often make the job of teaching slightly more manageable – but, as we have emphasised in the past, there is an important role for the teacher in reinforcing the messages associated with these tasks. This will further enhance feelings of worth. Additionally, teachers can look beyond the classroom for such opportunities. It is not unusual for schools to develop links with their communities, taking opportunities for activities which involve children doing good deeds and helping others. Examples we have experienced include schemes to help out citizens in the community who are unable to do their own shopping or tend their gardens, projects to help clean up areas of the neighbourhood, 'concert parties' to entertain older citizens in residential care, and so on. We discuss further aspects of citizenship in strategy 4 below.

Activity 1

Thinking about children's naturally occurring pro-social acts:

- How are these recognised in the class?
- What mechanisms are there for recognising caring and supportive behaviours in the wider school context?

Thinking about the idea of required helpfulness:

- To what extent do you look for opportunities to involve children in such activity?
- How might these be extended – both in the school and in the wider community?
- How might the self-worth messages be highlighted? Are there ways in which the teacher – and the school – might recognise and celebrate such behaviour?

Strategy 2: the value of peer tutoring

In a previous chapter, we considered how peer-assisted learning (PAL) in general can help pupils develop a sense of self-competence. Peer tutoring is one particular form of PAL and research has shown that this can have very definite benefits; these include learning gains, enhanced beliefs about competence and, of particular relevance to us here, gains in self-worth. It is important to note that the last of these, the gains in self-worth, seem to be particularly related to one type of peer tutoring: cross-age tutoring.

In Chapter 4, where we looked at research evidence on classroom processes, we briefly mentioned a recent study of paired reading in primary schools in Scotland (Miller et al., 2010). We noted that data collected indicated that children's sense of self-competence developed over the time of the research – for both tutors and tutees. Such gains are consistent with a picture of children recognising their improving skills, whether reading skills or tutoring skills (or both). However, we also highlighted that for one group in particular, there were gains in self-worth. This group comprised the cross-age tutors; that is, those older children who were tutors for younger children. Such findings seem to be consistent with beliefs, discussed above, about children gaining in feelings of worth from being placed in a position where they are helping others. As the authors of that study pointed out: 'The role of helping the young is one that is firmly embedded and respected in most cultures; cross-age peer tutoring is clearly an example of this' (p. 428).

The process of peer tutoring is somewhat more formal than some peer-assisted learning activities. Although peer tutoring can take many forms, it is perhaps best known in reading, where it is known as paired reading. Perhaps one reason for the popularity of this activity is the central role reading plays in children's learning in all curricular areas. It is often through reading that parents first judge how their child is performing at school. Many early years teachers will have experienced the anxious parent approaching the school to enquire about the 'reading book', particularly when it appears that their child did not get moved on to the next level book at the same time as others in the class. It is often in this area too that judgements are made about children's ability in general. From very early on in their school career, pressure is put on young learners, even by those who are not intending to do so, to succeed in this area. It is not surprising then that teachers have sought ways in which this success could be achieved by as many children as possible. Paired reading is one very effective tool in the learning-to-read armoury.

The work of Keith Topping gives an excellent insight into the theory and practice of paired reading: the preparation and the process as well as the theoretical background. Topping emphasises that successful projects do require some careful organisation on the part of the teacher. The arrangements for same-age tutoring are in many ways more straightforward than for cross-age tutoring, but bearing in mind the findings from the study referred to above (that it was *cross-age* tutoring that yielded the greatest gains in self-worth) we shall highlight the cross-age approach.

The procedure

The following outline of the general technique is based on Topping's method, as summarised in Miller, Topping and Thurston (2010):

> Pairs start by choosing books of high interest to themselves. These need to be above the independent readability level of the tutee, but not above that of the tutor. The children sit side-by-side so that they can both see the book comfortably. They are encouraged to talk about the book, to develop shared enthusiasm and ensure the tutee really understands the content. The tutor will read with the tutee at the start, and during difficult passages. While reading together, the tutor will modulate his or her speed to match that of the tutee, while giving a good model of competent reading. When an easier section of text is encountered, the tutee uses a pre-arranged signal; the tutor then stops reading out loud and the tutee reads alone. At some point, while reading alone the tutee is likely to make an error. Tutors do not immediately correct any mistakes; they pause for a specified time (in this case, four seconds) to allow time for tutee self-correction. If the tutee manages to self-correct, the tutor praises and the tutee continues reading alone. If the tutee is not able to self-correct within the specified time, the correction process is employed. The tutor (1) demonstrates the correct way to say the word, (2) has the tutee repeat it correctly, and (3) the pair continue – but reading together again now. When the tutee becomes confident again they can use the agreed signal to indicate they wish to read alone once more. The pair may alternate from reading together to reading alone many times during a session. Praise is an important element of the process, especially for correct reading of difficult words, getting all the words in a sentence right, and correcting errors before the tutor does. (p. 423)

Organisational aspects

The above overview applies to most forms of paired reading. However, with cross-age arrangements, there are some extra factors to take into account. Perhaps the first of these is to find a colleague who is interested in the approach and who will work consistently at this over a period of a term or so. When a suitable partner has been found, there is the question of how the sessions will be organised. One factor will be the time(s) of the week; this is usually one, two or three half-hour sessions per week. Other considerations will include deciding on the pairings, and the training for the children.

The advice from Topping is as follows. In cross-age tutoring, pupils in each class are ranked by reading ability, and the most able tutor in one class is matched with the most able tutee in the other class, the second best with the second, and so on. Small matching adjustments may be necessary on grounds of social compatibility. As a rule therefore, in cross-age tutoring the most able tutee is helped by the most able tutor; the weakest tutee is helped by the weakest older tutor. (As an aside, readers may not be surprised to learn that some of the biggest gains in self-esteem were achieved by the less-able tutors who were helping the less-able tutees.)

Pupils must also be aware not only of the process but of the rationale for using the strategy. They need to understand why they are paired together and how that pairing is going to assist in their learning. An appropriate time slot must also be clearly identified in the day and in the week when this activity can take place. On occasion, coordinating the timetables of two classes to ensure the cross-age element can prove a stumbling block – and is why some teachers prefer same-age tutoring. However, we would suggest that these difficulties *can* be overcome, particularly when both teachers believe in the benefits of paired reading with older children helping younger pupils.

Importantly, the sessions must be seen to be valued by those planning and organising the activity. When something gets moved about, or is easily postponed for another activity, it can send a message to children that this is not as important as other activities. This in turn can affect how the children themselves value the task. Although the process is straightforward and easily learned, some training is required for the pupils taking the role of tutor. This is sometimes done by teachers in role, acting out the process for the children, to support the learning of the skills. Once again, the environment of the classroom will have a part to play in this. In a classroom where children are used to hearing honest and relevant feedback, offered in a constructive and supportive manner, tutors will have seen appropriate behaviours being modelled.

Peer-assisted learning in general, and paired reading in particular, are amongst the most heavily researched techniques in mainstream education. There is no shortage of evidence that there are benefits for both the tutor and the tutee from the process; such benefits are both cognitive and affective. However, pupils – and particularly their parents – may need to have these benefits explained to them. Most will willingly accept the advantages to the tutee in practising a variety of reading skills, fluency, comprehension, word attack skills, and so on, whilst having the benefits of one-to-one support and encouragement. However, some may take persuasion that there are benefits for the child who is acting as tutor. The fact is that tutors can be fine-tuning their own skills in these areas, and as we pointed out in Chapter 5 with the story about Jerome Bruner, the task of explaining new knowledge to another can be a significant cognitive challenge (Bruner, 1963). In addition to these, we can add enhancing self-worth for tutors. At the risk of repetition, most children who are involved in this kind of activity believe that they are doing a good thing; it is good to help another.

Finally, we have focused here on a relatively straightforward – albeit a highly successful – form of peer tutoring. Topping and others have extended the work on paired reading into other areas, including paired thinking, paired maths and paired science (Thurston et al., 2009; Topping, 2001a, 2001b). But we wish to finish this section with some interesting work which has recently been conducted in the area of *reciprocal* peer tutoring. This is when individuals take on the role of tutor and tutee at different times. Some may be a little sceptical of such an approach, but an article by Thurston et al. (2009) reported an imaginative and worthwhile project involving reciprocal tutoring using ICT. This was briefly outlined in Chapter 5, but we repeat the main features here. Primary children in Scotland were tutoring children from a Spanish elementary school in English language, and in return the Scottish children were being tutored in their own learning of Spanish. Quite apart from the learning gains to be achieved here, one can see immediately the potential for benefits in terms of self-worth; children were being placed in a trusted role (effectively that of a teacher) and were providing help to other children who were relying on them to improve their learning of a new language.

Activity 2

If you use paired reading – or other forms of peer tutoring – in your classroom:

- What do you see as the main benefits?
- Can you see where some pupils have benefited from the experience in relation to their sense of self-worth – and if so, what might be the key processes at work?
- If there are cases where you do not see obvious signs that children are benefiting, can you identify the nature of the problem?
- How might these be overcome in order to take this forward with pupils? (It may be helpful to refer to the structural and organisational issues outlined above.)

If you do not use paired reading:

- Can you identify a colleague with whom you might work?
- What might be the main organisational issues to be considered?

Strategy 3: the role of behaviour codes

So far, we have been discussing pro-social behaviour: children doing things to help others. What about conduct more generally – everyday behaviour in the class and beyond? In essence, the line of reasoning here is consistent with what we have outlined above; if young children believe they are acting in a manner which is approved of, they will make self-appraisals that reflect feelings of worth. The bonus is that, subsequently, they are more likely to receive positive comments from others which reinforce such feelings. In practice, many teachers who have tried to help individuals to change negative behaviours will have experienced such processes operating from a different perspective. Children whose behaviour is anti-social or dysfunctional often experience uncertainty about their worth, and when their behaviour elicits unfavourable reaction from others, negative feelings of worth are further reinforced.

Of course, it has to be acknowledged that the situation is more complex than this, with a variety of social and cultural factors involved in such perceptions and evaluations; in particular, age and peer-group influences are mediating factors. Indeed, when negative labels become attached to children, and when children (sometimes, quite naturally) see other people as being biased against them, the situation can become even more complex and harder to address. However, the basic principle seems self-evidently true for most children of primary school age: self-worth reflects the extent to which children see themselves as being a 'good boy' or 'good girl' – and their behaviour is central to appraisals here.

What are the implications for a teacher's approach to behaviour management in class? Behaviour management policies come in many shapes and forms, from basic limit-setting approaches to those informed by humanism or systems theory. It is beyond the scope of this book to discuss the relative merits of the various alternatives; readers wishing to read more about the range of approaches and the beliefs and values which underpin them will find Louise Porter's book (2006) to be particularly helpful. Suffice it to say that the behaviour policies adopted by a school are influenced by a range of factors, most notably the values and beliefs of the school community. However, our message here is quite simple: in the interests of protecting and enhancing the self-worth of children, whatever system of behaviour management is employed, it is important that expectations are made very clear. The reason is equally simple – for children to make judgements about whether or not they are behaving well, they need to know what 'good behaviour' actually is.

Previous research (not to mention years of practitioner experience across many settings) tells us that while many children come to school already knowing what is expected in terms of conduct, a proportion do not. In some cases, children learn that the codes which apply in school are not the same as those they had previously known. For some, it is a long and difficult process to adapt to – and hopefully begin to internalise – the new codes. This process of adaptation is not neutral in its effects on an individual's self-worth; making the right or wrong decision about how to conduct oneself carries with it implications for whether individuals see themselves as good people or not. What makes this process more uncertain is if children are not sure what constitutes the 'right' behaviour in a given situation, particularly if this changes from day to day, or from context to context. In contrast, they can be helped to develop when they know exactly what the expected behaviour is, when these expectations are consistent, and when they receive honest feedback coupled with support and encouragement.

Many teachers appreciate that these three factors are central to effective behaviour management. What might not have been quite so obvious is that these same principles are important when thinking about how conduct and self-worth may be linked. Teachers – and schools – may base their behaviour policies on limit-setting approaches such as Assertive Discipline or Applied Behaviour Analysis at one end of the spectrum, right through to more democratic approaches, such as Choice Theory and Systems Theory at the other. Whereas the former tend to focus on order and compliance, the latter emphasise autonomy, emotional regulation and cooperation. But the point is this: whichever policy is adopted, if children are clear about what is considered desirable behaviour, if they find that these expectations are consistent amongst all adults within the school (and consistent over time) and if they receive appropriate and honest feedback about their conduct, then the policy employed is more likely to nurture self-worth.

One final point here: when discussing self-competence in previous chapters, we looked at contingent praise – praise that is related directly to achievement in a particular task or learning activity that children are involved in – and we discussed the value of being specific and relating that praise directly to performance in a given task. Although our focus is now on self-worth, the role of contingent praise should not be forgotten. It is particularly important when we are providing feedback on behaviour – whether in the form of praise for desirable behaviour or specific feedback and advice on unwanted behaviour. We need to ensure that children know what they are being praised for; this is important both for them, and for those who are watching and learning.

Activity 3

Thinking about the behaviour management system used in your school and/or in your class:

- What are the main beliefs and values which underpin it? Are any stated explicitly? If not, what do you see as the implicit values?
- Outline the main principles in practice – the key ideas that are stressed.

Now, thinking about the three features we have highlighted, reflect on the extent to which children are helped in the following respects:

- knowing exactly what the expected behaviour is
- ensuring these expectations are consistent
- providing honest feedback, support and encouragement about conduct.

In the light of your reflection here, what issues might be worthy of further discussion?

Strategy 4: looking to the curriculum for opportunities

A recurring message in the last four chapters of this book has been that we believe in enhancing self-esteem through regular activities which are ongoing features of mainstream life in classrooms. We are sceptical of 'special' self-esteem enhancing activities, however appealing, unless they have a convincing theoretical rationale; in our experience, few of them do. In this final section, we maintain this approach, and focus on ways in which we can use the formal curriculum to enhance self-worth. In essence, this involves looking at a curriculum area and considering the focus, the content and the associated activities to see whether there are opportunities for worth enhancement. We have chosen to illustrate this process with reference to three areas of the curriculum: citizenship activities, thinking skills and Religious and Moral Education (RME). However, these are used as examples, and we would encourage readers to explore beyond these in their own contexts.

In the UK, the introduction of the term 'citizenship' in schools can be traced back to the late 1990s. In different ways, the establishment of the Scottish parliament and the low turnout in the UK general election of 1999 both fuelled debates about participation and citizenship. This led naturally to the role of the school in developing citizenship, with two approaches being advocated. One was through the curriculum, with a separate subject area devoted to teaching how to be a good citizen (in some countries known as 'civics'). The other way was to develop an ethos of citizenship, giving children practical experience of 'being a citizen'. In practice, both the Scottish and English systems opted for a combination of these two approaches, albeit with slight differences in emphasis. The elements which make up the area of citizenship may vary from school to school, and indeed in more recent years the area has widened to include a 'global' element and issues of sustainable development.

At a very general level, it can be seen that work in the area of citizenship can bring benefits in both competence and worth. Like most subjects, the competence element can be enhanced by effective teaching and the acquisition of new knowledge and skills; as we noted in an earlier chapter, the fact that the learning is seen as authentic and relevant to children may help in this respect. However, in the case of citizenship activities, the benefits in terms of competence can be on a wider scale. When children become engaged in practical projects in the community, the activities, if well managed, provide a wider range of opportunities to meet new challenges and learn and apply new skills. Children who may not excel at academic tasks may be effective contributors in practical tasks and in tackling problems of a different type. But – and returning to the main focus of this chapter – because of the nature of many community projects, children can also benefit in terms of worth; they are engaged in doing good work for others. They are helping individuals, or groups, or the community as a whole – and should be recognised for this work.

Readers will already be aware of a wide variety of experiences for pupils. These range from the local level – for example, visits to senior citizens' clubs for carol concerts, or arranging daffodil teas where the community come into the school to be entertained – to sponsored school events to raise money for national events such as Comic Relief or in response to natural disasters on a global scale, such as the tsunami in 2011. Other examples we know of include classes which have taken responsibility for the upkeep of part of the grounds at an old-folks' home and several community-based projects involving improving playgrounds, nature walks and local streams. Many schools now play an active role in the community in which they are situated; but in many cases this has been extended to a national or international level. In fact, it is now commonplace for the global dimension to be added to citizenship and this can often follow the pattern of the younger pupils looking to their own local community, slightly older classes taking a more national approach and the older pupils looking at the global perspective. Such a development is consistent with many beliefs about the development of understanding as children move through school. From our self-worth perspective, this work opens up many more opportunities for children to be engaged in tasks which involve helping others.

The idea of sustainable development is another important element of citizenship in schools. Certainly, 'taking care of the environment' was always an important aspect of work with children in school; respect for the environment, not dropping litter, taking care of school gardens and re-cycling materials in and out of school were all part of encouraging pupils to engage with and take a pride in their environment. By enabling pupils to see that they can make effective changes in that environment, teachers can give pupils a sense of control (which can also influence beliefs about competence and ownership). This aspect of citizenship has developed to include much more sophisticated ways of looking at the world and its resources, as well as issues of fair trade. In essence then, pupils are dealing with far more complex issues than simply keeping the playground tidy. Considering how they and their parents shop, how the trainers they are wearing were made or the way in which food is produced and sold brings difficult issues to the attention of children in an authentic manner. In many ways, this is empowering and, as is usually the case with our children, their sense of fairness enables them to develop an understanding of the world in which they live. Such topics can be challenging for pupils but, with careful handling on the part of school staff, children can grow and make considered choices which will make them feel good about themselves as contributors to society and enhance their sense of self-worth. The caveat here – of course – is that the teacher has to handle discussion of the issues with care and sensitivity. Luckily for teachers, some excellent literature has recently been produced in this area, and even more is available online (see the Further reading section at the end of this chapter).

The idea of democracy is most certainly a key element of citizenship; on different levels the curriculum and ethos of the school will enable pupils to appreciate that they have a right to their individual opinion. This relates clearly to some of the discussion in Chapter 7. Democracy in action is often witnessed through a 'pupil council' where children from each class are elected to represent their peers on the group and to have their say about the running of the school. Although in the early days of pupil councils the range of topics could be fairly limited, and often centred on school meals and the condition of the toilets, the agendas have become much more sophisticated. Often, the councils now have a say in much more fundamental school issues to do with resources and learning and, in some instances, the appointment of staff. When pupils have their voices listened to and acted upon, and they can see the evidence of that action in their class or school, they have a much stronger sense of belonging to the community. This sense of belonging in itself can further enhance self-worth.

To recap here: it is very evident that citizenship education involves many constructive and altruistic activities; but it also involves the exploration of associated issues, often based around values such as equity, compassion and justice. Through supporting children in their understanding and appreciation of such matters, in a manner which is appropriate to their age and stage of development, teachers can open up many opportunities for self-worth enhancement. But citizenship is not the only area of the curriculum where there is potential when considering 'doing the right thing' or 'leading a good life'. One of these is the area known variously as philosophical thinking or thinking skills.

In fact, there are many links between philosophical thinking and active citizenship, in the sense that learning to think clearly – and convey your ideas effectively and confidently – helps the process of engaging with other people and other communities. Importantly, it is another area of the curriculum where we may see opportunities to encourage self-worth through helping children towards more thoughtful and virtuous behaviour. The *Philosophy for Children* (P4C) approach is built around the notion of a 'community of inquiry' – a group of learners who, over time, build a community which shares a collaborative and reflective approach to discussion. Its purpose is to encourage cooperation, care and respect – all qualities which have a bearing on the issues we have discussed earlier related to positive behaviours. Emphasis is placed on understanding and meaning, truth and discussion of values; again, we see opportunities for teachers to make links with the idea of virtuous conduct, discussed earlier.

Indeed, in the course of the P4C sessions, there is an emphasis on developing skills of self-management. Children are encouraged to listen to each other and respect everyone's ideas. One of the main principles of P4C is *reasonableness* – in terms of the way children conduct themselves in sessions, in being open to new ideas, taking time to consider differing points of view and valuing those arguments that are supported by reasons. Following the line of argument we outlined earlier in this chapter, developing such skills and attitudes can bring benefits for children in terms of self-worth because they can encourage positive ways of behaving and relating to others.

Activities typical of P4C include encouraging and developing questioning skills, helping children to discuss and develop concepts, and encouraging dialogue and argument (though of an exploratory rather than adversarial nature). P4C sequences typically involve the teacher in the following steps: preparing the context (for example, the physical layout and guidelines for interaction); preparing the text (although 'texts' can be images or artefacts, as well as text-based material); preparing for progression (reflecting on what to encourage or emphasise, and anticipating possible interventions); sharing the text (presenting the material in such a way that it engages the children); creating and choosing questions (pupils are encouraged to create questions that lead to a good dialogue); dialogue (this is the key part of the session, and an important message is that it focuses on building something together, rather than exchanging ready-made opinions); and follow-up (considering a plan for further development of the dialogue, such as highlighting a concept or behaviour to explore at a later stage). For more detail on these processes, see the Further reading.

Finally here, when discussing values, attitudes and beliefs, it is clear that the RME curriculum is useful for the teacher keen to look for opportunities for self-worth enhancement. Although different education authorities and schools may differ in their approach to the RME curriculum, common elements tend to include an emphasis on helping children to understand and value religious and cultural diversity, both within their own local communities and further afield. There is also a focus on proactive acts, with children encouraged to participate in service to others. Once again, we see links here with the development of self-worth through virtuous conduct.

To illustrate potential links with self-worth, we have extracted some statements from the official Scottish curriculum guidelines, *Religious and Moral Education: Principles and Practice* (Scottish Government, 2009a, p. 1):

Learning through religious and moral education enables children and young people to:

- develop respect for others and an understanding of beliefs and practices which are different from their own
- explore and establish values such as wisdom, justice, compassion and integrity and engage in the development of and reflection upon their own moral values

- develop their beliefs, attitudes, values and practices through reflection, discovery and critical evaluation
- develop the skills of reflection, discernment, critical thinking and deciding how to act when making moral decisions
- make a positive difference to the world by putting their beliefs and values into action.

To further illustrate the point, the following outcomes have been extracted from the sister document, *Religious and Moral Education: Experiences and Outcomes* (Scottish Government, 2009b, p. 2ff.):

- I can share my developing views about values such as fairness and equality and love, caring, sharing and human rights. (RME 2–02a)
- I can demonstrate my developing understanding of moral values through participating in events and projects which make a positive difference to others. (RME 3–05b)
- I can apply my developing understanding of morality to consider a range of moral dilemmas in order to find ways which could promote a more just and compassionate society. (RME 4–05b)
- I am developing my own understanding of values such as honesty, respect and compassion and am able to identify how these values might be applied in relation to moral issues. (RME 3–09b)

These extracts are from the official guidance in one country; while they will differ from policies in other countries and regions, it is likely that many of the core values and concerns are shared. Returning to our principal focus, readers who have followed the argument about the links between beliefs, conduct and self-worth so far will be aware of the opportunities which are created when children are engaged in work related to RME.

To reiterate the key message in this section: we have briefly looked at some features of citizenship, thinking skills and RME to illustrate a fundamental point. There are opportunities within the formal curriculum which can be useful in our attempts to nurture and enhance the self-worth of pupils. None of them is *guaranteed* to do so, of course – hardly surprising, since the primary purpose in each case is related to 'academic' learning, not self-worth enhancement. If teachers do not see the potential that exists, or if they fail to relate such messages to a self-worth agenda, then the chance will pass them by: a missed opportunity for them and their children. On the other hand, a teacher who sees the potential, and then uses her psychological and pedagogical knowledge to make links, creates opportunities to enhance pupils' beliefs about acceptance and virtue.

Activity 4

Take one of the examples above – citizenship, RME or thinking skills:

- Note down some of the key learning experiences you hope children will benefit from in this area of the curriculum.
- Now, identify any activities which you believe have the potential to enhance self-worth. Can you articulate why this is so?
- How might these activities be further developed?

Now choose one other area of the curriculum (or any classroom activity) in which the children are routinely engaged:

- Identify any issues that might have a bearing on children's ideas about 'doing the right thing'.
- How might these issues be explored; what activities could the children be engaged in?

Chapter summary and conclusion

William James (1890/1983), often considered the father of self-esteem, famously claimed that 'The deepest principle in human nature is the craving to be appreciated' (James, 1920 (n.p)). One suspects that this claim, made in the 1890s, is as true in today's tech-savvy, materialistic and highly competitive society as it was then. As teachers, it is natural for us to want others to feel good about themselves – and this is particularly the case with the children we teach. However, what we have been trying to promote in the last two chapters is the value of giving children real opportunities and experiences for this to happen. Teachers are unlikely to build a robust sense of worth in their pupils through self-esteem 'experiences' where children are asked to tell peers what they are good at, or colour in pictures that form the words 'I am special' – just two of the activities which have been advocated in the past.

However, by thinking about the processes through which a person's self-worth is influenced over time, and the central role of conduct as a focus of messages and evaluations in this respect, we can appreciate the potential here. By recognising children's caring or thoughtful acts when they occur, by further encouraging pro-social behaviour through processes such as required helpfulness, by harnessing the power of peer tutoring, by supporting children in making good choices in terms of conduct and by seeing the possibilities in various curricular activities, we can provide opportunities for children to experience a sense of worth. It is when such experiences are genuine and meaningful – and when caring and informed teachers support and reinforce the messages that are created, consistently over a period of time – that we may realistically hope to enhance the self-worth of our pupils.

Some important tips

Do	Don't
• Be aware of occasions when children act in a caring or considerate way; ensure you highlight these	• Let pro-social acts, and those responsible for them, go unrecognised
• Be on the alert for stories of pro-social acts from the playground, dinner hall, etc.	• Concern yourself only with what goes on within your classroom
• Look for opportunities to create tasks based on the idea of 'required helpfulness'	• Underestimate the extent to which such tasks can influence children's perceptions of worth
• Allow children to discuss and explore their experiences and feelings in such tasks	• Ignore such opportunities for discussion because these tasks seem unimportant in educational terms
• Try to reinforce the worth-enhancing messages which accompany such activities	• Assume this is not an important part of your role
• Learn more about the possibilities provided by peer tutoring – particularly of younger children	• Limit any peer work to cooperative group work in your own class
• Work with a colleague of a younger class to overcome any organisational difficulties	• Assume that the organisation of cross-age tutoring will be too difficult
• Monitor the progress of the matched pairs, especially in the early stages	• Assume that the skills of tutoring will come naturally
• Explore the opportunities provided by reciprocal peer tutoring	• Dismiss reciprocal peer tutoring as an unrealistic proposition in primary classes
• Appreciate that the way children conduct themselves can have an effect on feelings of worth	• Dismiss behaviour as having nothing to do with self-esteem
• Support good behaviour by providing clear expectations and being consistent in your approach	• Underestimate the value of providing clear expectations for children and reinforcing these
• Focus on reinforcing good behaviour: 'catch them being good'	• Focus on the negative – on sanctions and demerits
• Be honest, but constructive, in responding to unwanted behaviour; for many children it is part of a learning process	• Assume that it's not your job to support behaviour – children should know how to behave and what is expected of them in class
• Accentuate the positive – but it is equally important to label clearly any undesirable behaviour	• Ignore bad behaviour (except in very specific cases and for a very specific reason)
• In such cases, label the behaviour, not the child	• Fall into the trap of labelling the child as troublesome or 'naughty'
• Remember to reinforce pro-social behaviour by 'catching them doing good'	• Miss out on opportunities to praise children for demonstrating kindness and thoughtfulness to others

Do	Don't
• Consider all areas of the 'academic' curriculum for their potential for discussing worth-based issues	• View learning experiences solely in terms of knowledge to be transmitted
• Emphasise any worth-based messages which emerge in these different curricular areas	• Allow such messages to pass by, or assume children will automatically make connections
• Look at a range of issues related to citizenship, such as how pupils can effect change by their own actions	• Allow pupils to believe that citizenship activity is *only* about doing charitable work
• Use work in the area of P4C and RME to discuss values and beliefs which underpin caring and pro-social actions	• View these areas of the curriculum solely in terms of their knowledge and skills
• Use language that helps children understand the issues, and how their contribution is valued	• Use jargon and catchphrases where the meaning is unclear to the children

Further reading

1. For more about children 'doing good' and pro-social behaviour, see:
- Bierhoff, H-W. (2002) *Pro-social Behaviour*. Hove: Psychology Press.
- Tanner, R.E.S. (2007) *Social Behaviour of Children*. New Delhi: Concept Publishing.

2. For more on peer tutoring, see:
- Thurston, A., Duran, B., Cunningham, E., Blanch, S. & Topping, K.J. (2009) International on-line reciprocal peer tutoring to promote modern language development in primary schools. *Computers & Education*, 53, 462–72.
- Topping, K.J. (2001a) *Peer Assisted Learning. A Practical Guide for Teachers*. Cambridge, MA: Brookline Books.
- Topping, K.J. (2001b) *Thinking, Reading, Writing: A Practical Guide to Paired Learning with Peers, Parents and Volunteers*. London: Continuum.

3. For more on behaviour management, see:
- Ellis, S. & Tod, J. (2009) *Behaviour for Learning*. Oxon: Routledge.
- Porter, L. (2006) *Behaviour in Schools*. Buckingham: Open University Press.

4. For more on using the curriculum to provide opportunities, see:
For citizenship:
- Barnickle, C. & Wilson, D. (2000) *Me as a Citizen*. Leamington Spa: Hopscotch.
- Collins, M. (2008) *Global Citizenship for Young Children*. London: Sage.
For philosophy:
- Fisher, R. (1996) *Stories for Thinking*. Oxford: Nash Pollock.
- The Philosophy for Children website at: www.philosophyforchildren.co.uk/
- The SAPERE website (communities of enquiry) at: www.sapere.org.uk/

Conclusion

In this short concluding chapter, we recap briefly on some key points, acknowledge areas where we have, of necessity, been selective in our focus, and conclude with two important messages. The first of these concerns how people see the relationship between school attainment and self-esteem. The second sounds a note of caution about over-reacting to some of the errors of the past; in a sense, it is a warning about the dangers of educational fashion. Our final word is one of affirmation for the teacher.

The key messages

Essentially, this book is anchored by a simple belief: we are more likely to be able to enhance self-esteem in the class if we become better informed about what it is and how it 'works'. Such knowledge should move us beyond an endless search for feel-good messages and a culture of constant praise. Nicholas Emler makes a similar point in the conclusion to his review of the evidence on self-esteem:

> a well-founded understanding of the phenomenon one is trying to change will produce more effective efforts than facile intuitions of the 'positive feedback – good, negative feedback – bad' variety that permeate the self-esteem industry. (Emler, 2001, p. 60)

In order to gain that well-founded understanding of the phenomenon, we have adopted a two-dimensional model of self-esteem. We have done so because it has several advantages for teachers. As we explained in earlier chapters, it is able to incorporate many important findings from decades of quite diverse research in the field.

> A balanced understanding of the nature and importance of both dimensions [competence and worth] would go far in reconciling seemingly discrepant perspectives and preventing future inconsistencies. The result promises to be a clearer account of what is arguably our most important attitude. (Tafarodi and Milne, 2002, p. 476)

Importantly, it does so in a coherent manner which seems in tune with the experience of primary teachers. The theory tells us that an individual's level of self-esteem reflects the integrated sum of two judgements: beliefs about competence and feelings of worth. It provides a helpful conceptual framework – a lens through which we can view, and evaluate, many aspects of classroom practice. In effect, it helps us to see the wood as well as the trees.

Accordingly, we looked at some basic ideas related to self-competence, emphasising that it is developed by new achievements: by success in meeting challenges. We discussed several techniques which teachers can use in the class to increase the likelihood of children improving their performance. We also spent some time looking at the beliefs which children (and teachers) have about learning, intelligence and motivation. Understanding such beliefs, and how we can influence them, helps in our quest to encourage better attitudes to learning – and consequently levels of achievement.

We then focused on self-worth, looking at a range of techniques that teachers can use to help children feel that they are accepted and valued for who they are. We looked at intrinsic worth and also at the ways in which children's conduct influences how they feel about themselves. We suggested that teachers can help by encouraging and recognising 'good' courses of action. In discussing worth-based strategies – as with those related to competence – we have offered practical advice which we hope teachers will find useful for their own contexts.

Errors of omission or commission?

Given the size of the field, it is inevitable that some readers may feel that an important aspect of theory has been ignored, or some useful classroom technique overlooked. An example of the former might be the work on self-worth protection, where researchers have been investigating links between decision making and perceptions of self-worth. On the other hand, we may have included aspects of theory or practice which readers feel are less helpful. As we explained in Chapter 2, the field of self-esteem is varied, the theoretical literature wide-ranging, research perspectives diverge and many beliefs are contested. Our aim has been to fashion a path through this material – a path which teachers will see as relevant to their own experience. We would argue that the rationale for the book, the way we have summarised the theory and research in the area, and the way in which the two-dimensional model has been used consistently to identify strategies and techniques, should help the reader along that path. Additionally, we hope that the advice contained within these chapters will help avoid some potential wrong turnings along the way.

Those readers with longer memories may recall some of these wrong turnings. A previous generation of 'self-esteem activities' tended to major on commercial worksheets or 'fun' activities designed to simulate and sustain a culture of compliments. The belief was that these would produce an instant boost to children's self-esteem – making them feel special, capable and worthwhile. It will be noted that no such quick fixes have appeared in this book. There is a good reason for this, quite apart from any reservations about the activities themselves. It is accepted that self-esteem can be resistant to change; it changes slowly and, sometimes, reluctantly. It is unlikely to be enhanced by some superficially appealing but short-term message – particularly one which becomes lost in the bigger picture of children's day-to-day lives. In reality, it is the lived experience of everyday events – facing challenges, receiving authentic messages from others, feeling cared for or neglected, making comparisons, being recognised or ignored, acting in one way rather than another – which forms the raw data on which judgements of self-esteem are based. If, as teachers, we appreciate this and use this knowledge to inform the way we manage learning and interact with children, and do so *consistently* over time, we increase our chances of making a difference.

One area that might have benefited from further exploration is the relationship between the two components of self-esteem. We have maintained the distinction between self-competence and self-worth throughout, in the interest of clarity. However, as with most theories in the social sciences, there are some interesting anomalies, and in reality the truth is messier than this. For example, as Tafarodi, Marshall and Milne (2003) point out, at times a specific competence can be celebrated as a virtue – something which is inherently good and contributes to feelings of worth. Equally, at times, qualities of character which are essentially good can be used by an individual for instrumental purposes – that is, they can contribute to feelings of competence.

At a more practical level, some of the techniques we have described can influence both dimensions of self-esteem. To illustrate, with peer tutoring, tutors develop skills of supporting their tutees' learning and recognise they know more about their topic than those they are helping (competence factors); but they also benefit from knowing that they are helping others (a worth-enhancing process). Another example is provided by citizenship activities, which can also involve both types of message. In fact, in our discussion of conduct, we concentrated mainly on its relationship with feelings of worth; but it would be equally valid to look at behaviour from the perspective of competence, for example, in terms of inter-personal and intra-personal skills.

Despite these examples, which appear to blur boundaries in some instances, the fundamental distinction between the two components of self-esteem is clear and well supported. Indeed, understanding this can help teachers to appreciate the full extent of some particularly worrying situations in relation to self-esteem. One of these is when ambitious parents place so much emphasis on academic achievement that children see parental affection as being dependent on them performing (more accurately, outperforming others) in school. That is, worth – even love – becomes conditional on competence. In this context, you may recall Mruk's (1999) work on defensive self-esteem, discussed in Chapter 3. Teachers who have experienced children being placed under such pressures will be able to testify to the potential for harm here. From a self-esteem perspective, in this situation if a child is not achieving the goals set for him, he suffers in two respects; not only is a sense of competence under threat, so too is the extent to which he feels worthy of love and affection.

This leads into areas which merit further investigation. It follows from the preceding paragraphs that it would be valuable to look in more detail at those situations when worth and competence interact with each other. Another area that we feel is of interest concerns the teacher's psychological and pedagogical knowledge – and how this helps to guide self-esteem enhancement strategies. There has been much theorising about how teachers and student teachers combine their knowledge of academic subject matter with their pedagogical skills to teach effectively (see, for example, Shulman's work [1986, 1987] where he discusses subject matter knowledge [SMK] and pedagogical content knowledge [PCK]). In contrast, the relationship between psychological and pedagogical knowledge and the affective side of education has received little attention. When thinking about self-esteem enhancement – and indeed personal and social education more broadly – this seems to us to be an issue which merits closer attention.

Two concluding messages

We finish with two brief messages; one may seem almost self-evident, the other possibly less so. The first is that, in much of the debate about self-esteem, children's academic attainment and self-esteem enhancement have been seen as competing demands on a teacher's time. One of the central arguments of the anti-self-esteem lobby was that teachers were devoting much precious time to self-esteem activities, time that would be better spent on 'real' academic learning. The counter-argument from pro-self-esteemers was that time spent on enhancing self-esteem would lead to greater self-belief, which would eventually result in improved attainment. We discussed the research evidence in this area in earlier chapters. But the point here is that implicit in the argument was a belief that the two processes were different in nature; a teacher focused *either* on enhancing self-esteem *or* she focused on improving learning. The two-dimensional model of self-esteem illustrates, most clearly through its focus on self-competence, how self-esteem and learning are developed simultaneously. As we have emphasised at many points, beliefs about self-competence are based on genuine achievements – essentially success in meeting challenges – and not least in academic learning. Hopefully this realisation may help to bring together teachers who were previously divided over the subject of self-esteem. One suspects that it may also help management teams in schools to achieve a consensus on moving forward policy in this area.

The second message sounds a note of caution. Although there is evidence that the importance of self-competence is now being recognised (often in the guise of self-efficacy), there are signs that it is being promoted as an *alternative* to self-esteem. This was exemplified at a recent conference in Glasgow[1] where a group of respected academics and social commentators took a critical look at self-esteem, articulating many of the accepted arguments against the more extreme self-esteem practices which we touched upon in our introduction. While this was a stimulating and thought-provoking session, it became apparent that the alternative being offered to self-esteem was a combination of self-efficacy and optimism (Craig, 2010). Leaving aside for a moment the issue of optimism, the problem for us lies in the absence of the other dimension of self-esteem: the belief that one has an intrinsic worth – that one is entitled to happiness, and to care and respect from others, irrespective of one's abilities. In our drive to emphasise competence, should we – *can* we – ignore this aspect of an individual's self-beliefs?

We believe there may be a danger here. A characteristic of a previous generation of self-esteem policies and books for teachers was that they tended to focus only on one dimension of self-esteem: in that case, self-worth. Indeed, even a cursory examination of self-esteem books for teachers over the past 25 years indicates that most activities were designed to make children feel better about themselves as individuals; few looked at the development of competence to any extent. But healthy self-esteem involves both elements; it is the belief that one is competent to cope *and* worthy of happiness. There is an issue of balance. We must not lose sight of the distortions produced in some contexts when we became fixated only on one dimension of self-esteem.

In 1905, the Spanish-American philosopher, George Santayana, issued a warning that 'those who cannot remember the past are condemned to repeat it'. Those who remember, but are unable to make the connection, are equally at risk.

The last word: over to you

Writing a book is a developmental process, in more ways than one, and as we worked on the later chapters, particularly those related to self-worth, we became increasingly convinced of one fundamental point. We mentioned it in the conclusion to Chapter 7, but it bears repeating here. The strategies and techniques we have described are not the most important factors here; none of them can be *guaranteed* to enhance self-esteem. This is particularly so when talking about nurturing self-worth, but it also applies to many of the self-competence techniques. It is the teacher who holds the key. A teacher with a sound understanding of self-esteem is more likely to *see the potential* that exists within an activity for the enhancement of worth and competence. If she then maximises that potential by reinforcing the self-esteem messages as appropriate, she is doing all she can to nurture the self-esteem of those for whom she is responsible.

The fact that you have stayed with us to the end of the final chapter suggests that you have a commitment to helping your pupils in this way. We hope that the content and the structure of this book will help to guide you in your endeavours.

Notes

1 The Centre for Confidence and Wellbeing, 30.3.2010

References

Ager, R. (2008) *Information and Communications Technology in Primary Schools: Children or Computers in Control?* 2nd edn. Oxon: Routledge.

Argyle, M. (1969) *Social Interaction.* London: Methuen.

Aristotle (2009) *The Nichomachean Ethics*, D. Ross and L. Brown, trans. Oxford: Oxford University Press.

Barnickle, C. & Wilson, D. (2000) *Me as a Citizen.* Leamington Spa: Hopscotch.

Baumeister, R.F., Campbell, J.D., Krueger, J.I. & Vohs, K.D. (2003) Does high self-esteem cause better performance, interpersonal success, happiness or healthier lifestyles? *Psychological Science in the Public Interest*, 4 (1), 1–44.

Bierhoff, H-W. (2002) *Pro-social Behaviour.* Hove: Psychology Press.

Black, P. & Wiliam, D. (2001) *Inside the Black Box: Raising Standards Through Classroom Assessment.* London: School of Education, King's College London.

Branden, N. (1969) *The Psychology of Self-esteem.* New York: Bantam Books.

Branden, N. (1994) *The Six Pillars of Self-esteem.* New York: Bantam Books.

Brown, M. (2009) *Personal, Social and Emotional Development.* Carlton: Curriculum Corporation.

Byron, T. (2008) *Safer Children in a Digital World: The Report of the Byron Review.* Department for Children, Schools and Families. Available at: www.dfes.gov. uk/byronreview/pdfs/Final%20Report%20Bookmarked.pdf

California State Department of Education (1992) *Toward a State of Esteem: The Final Report of the California Task Force to Promote Self-esteem and Personal and Social Responsibility.* Available at: www.eric.ed.gov/PDFS/ED321170.pdf

Canfield, J. & Wells, H.C. (1994) *100 Ways to Enhance Self-Concept in the Primary Classroom.* Boston, MA: Allyn & Bacon.

Canter, L. & Canter, M. (1992) *Lee Canter's Assertive Discipline: Positive Behavior Management for Today's Classroom.* Santa Monica, CA: Canter & Associates.

Cheminais, R. (2008) *Engaging Pupil Voice to Ensure that Every Child Matters: A Practical Guide.* London: David Fulton.

Cigman, R. (2001) Self-esteem and the confidence to fail. *Journal of Philosophy of Education*, 35 (4), 561–76.

Clarke, S. (2001) *Unlocking Formative Assessment: Practical Strategies for Enhancing Pupils' Learning in the Primary Classroom.* London: Hodder and Stoughton.

Collins, M. (2008) *Global Citizenship for Young Children.* London: Sage.

Condie, R. & Munro, B. (2007) *The Impact of ICT in Schools: A Landscape Review.*

Coventry: Becta.

Cooley, C.H. (1902) *Human Nature and the Social Order*. New York: C. Scribner.

Coopersmith, S. (1967) *The Antecedents of Self-esteem*. San Francisco, CA: Freeman.

Covington, M.V. (1992) *Making the Grade: A Self-Worth Perspective on Motivation and School Reform*. Cambridge, MA: Cambridge University Press.

Covington, M.V. (2001) The science and politics of self-esteem: schools caught in the middle. In T.J. Owens, S. Stryker & N. Goodman (eds) *Extending Self-Esteem Theory and Research*. New York: Cambridge University Press.

Craig, C. (2010) Self-esteem. Paper presented at the Conference on self-esteem: the facts, myths, challenges and alternatives. Centre for Confidence and Wellbeing Glasgow, 30 March 2010.

Crocker, J. & Wolfe, C.T. (2001) Contingencies of self-worth. *Psychological Review*, 108 (3), 593–623.

Csíkszentmihályi, M. (1990) *Flow: The Psychology of Optimal Experience*. New York: Harper Collins.

Curry, M. & Bromfield, C. (1994) *Personal and Social Education for Primary Schools through Circle Time*. Tamworth: NASEN.

Damon, W. (1995) *Greater Expectations: Overcoming the Culture of Indulgence in our Homes and Schools*. New York: The Free Press.

Dowling, M. (2009) *Young Children's Personal, Social and Emotional Development*. London: Sage.

Dweck, C.S. (1999) *Self-theories: Their Role in Motivation, Personality and Development*. Philadelphia, PA: Psychology Press.

Dweck, C.S. (2007) *Mindset: The New Psychology of Success*. New York: Ballantine Books.

Elliott, J. (2002) Could do better? The risks of cultivating positive self-esteem. *Human Givens*, 9 (1), 38–43.

Ellis, S. & Tod, J. (2009) *Behaviour for Learning*. Oxon: Routledge.

Emler, N. (2001) *Self-Esteem: The Costs and Causes of Low Self-Worth*. York: Joseph Rowntree Foundation and YPS.

Epstein, S. (1979) The ecological study of emotions in humans. In P. Pliner, K.R. Blankstein & I.M. Spigel (eds) *Advances in the Study of Communication and Affect, Vol. 5: Perception of Emotions in Self and Others*. New York: Plenum.

Festinger, L. (1954). A theory of social comparison processes. *Human Relations*, 7 (2), 117–40.

Fisher, R. (1996) *Stories for Thinking*. Oxford: Nash Pollock.

Flutter, J. & Rudduck, J. (2004) *Consulting Pupils: What's in it for Schools?* London: RoutledgeFalmer.

Fox, R. (2005) *Teaching and Learning: Lessons from Psychology*. Oxford: Blackwell.

Gee, J.P. (2003) *What Video Games Have to Teach Us About Learning and Literacy*. London: Palgrave.

Goleman, D. (1995) *Emotional Intelligence*. New York: Bantam Books.

Gutterige, D. & Smith, V. (2005) *Using Circle Time for PSHE and Citizenship: A Year's Plan for Key Stage 2 Teachers*. Oxford: David Fulton.

Harter, S. (1985) *Manual for the Self-Perception Profile for Children*. Denver, CO: University of Denver.

Harter, S. (1990) Self and identity development. In S. Shirley & G. Elliot (eds) *At the Threshold: The Developing Adolescent*. Cambridge, MA: Harvard University Press.

Harter, S. (2011) *The Construction of the Self: Developmental and Sociocultural*, 2nd edn. New York: Guilford Press.

Hewitt, J.P. (1998) *The Myth of Self-esteem: Finding Happiness and Solving Problems in America*. New York: St Martin's Press.

Humphrey, N., Kalambouka, A., Bolton, J., Lendrum, A., Wigelsworth, M., Lennie, C. & Farrell, P. (2008) *Primary Social and Emotional Aspects of Learning (SEAL) Evaluation of Small Group Work*. Nottingham: DCSF Publications.

James, W. (1890/1983) *The Principles of Psychology*. Cambridge, MA: Harvard University Press.

James, W. (1920) Familiar letters of William James. *The Atlantic Monthly*, August 1920. Available at: www.theatlantic.com/past/docs/issues/96may/nitrous/jamii.htm (accessed 6 November 2011).

Jindal-Snape, D. & Miller D.J. (2008) A challenge of living? Understanding the psycho-social processes of the child during primary–secondary transition through resilience and self-esteem theories. *Educational Psychology Review*, 20 (3), 217–36.

Johnston, J., Halocha, J. & Chater, M. (2007) *Developing Teaching Skills in the Primary School*. Maidenhead: Open University Press.

Kohn, A. (1994) The truth about self-esteem. *Phi Delta Kappan*, 76, 272–83.

Kohn, A. (1996) *Beyond Discipline: From Compliance to Community*. Alexandria, VA: ASCD.

Lawrence, D. (2006) *Enhancing Self-esteem in the Classroom*, 3rd edn. London: Sage.

Leary, M.R. (1999) Making sense of self-esteem. *Current Directions in Psychological Science*, 8 (1), 32–5.

McLean, A. (2001) Have we got it wrong about self-esteem? *Times Educational Supplement Scotland*, 16 March.

McLean, A. (2003) *The Motivated School*. London: Sage.

McLean, A. (2009) *Motivating Every Learner*. London: Sage.

McNamara, S. & Moreton, G. (1997) *Understanding Differentiation: A Teacher's Guide*. London: David Fulton.

Marsh, H.W. (1992) *Self Description Questionnaire (SDQ) I: A theoretical and empirical basis for the measurement of multiple dimensions of pre-adolescent self-concept*. An interim test manual and research monograph. Macarthur, NSW: University of Western Sydney, Faculty of Education.

Marsh, H.W. (2008) The elusive importance effect: more failure for the Jamesian perspective on the importance of importance in shaping self-esteem. *Journal of Personality*, 76 (5), 1081–122.

Marsh, H.W. & Craven, R.G. (2006) Reciprocal effects of self-concept and performance from a multidimensional perspective. *Perspectives on Psychological Science*, 1 (2), 133–66.

Merton, R. (1957) *Social Theory and Social Structure*. New York: Free Press.

Miller, D.J. & Daniel, B. (2007) Competent to cope, worthy of happiness? How the duality of self-esteem can inform a resilience-based classroom environment. *School Psychology International*, 28 (5), 605–22.

Miller D.J. & Lavin, F.M. (2007) 'But now I feel I want to give it a try': formative assessment, self-esteem and a sense of competence. *The Curriculum Journal*, 18 (1), 3–25.

Miller, D.J. & Moran, T.R. (2007) Theory and practice in self-esteem enhancement: circle-time and efficacy-based approaches – a controlled evaluation. *Teachers and Teaching: Theory and Practice*, 13 (6), 601–15.

Miller, D.J. & Robertson, D.P. (2010) Using a games console in the primary classroom: effects of 'brain training' programme on computation and self-esteem. *British Journal of Educational Technology*, 41(2), 242–55.

Miller, D.J., Topping, K.J. & Thurston, A. (2010) Peer tutoring in reading: the effects of role and organization on two dimensions of self-esteem. *British Journal of Educational Psychology*, 80, 417–33.

Mosley, J. (1993) *Turn Your School Round*. Cambridge: LDA.

Mosley, J. (1996) *Quality Circle Time in the Primary Classroom*. Cambridge: LDA.

Mosley, J. (1998) *More Quality Circle Time*. Cambridge: LDA.

Mruk, C. (1999) *Self-esteem: Research, Theory and Practice*. London: Free Association Books.

Newman, T. (2004) *What Works in Building Resilience*. Ilford: Barnardo's.

Nolte, D. (1998) *Children Learn What They Live: Parenting to Inspire Values*. New York: Workman Publishing.

November, A. (2010) *Empowering Students with Technology*, 2nd edn. Thousand Oaks, CA: Corwin.

O'Brien, E.J. & Epstein, S. (1983) *The Multidimensional Self-Esteem Inventory*. Odessa, FL: Psychological Assessment Resources.

O'Brien, T. & Guiney, D. (2001) *Differentiation in Teaching and Learning*. London: Continuum.

Porter, L. (2006) *Behaviour in Schools*. Buckingham: Open University Press.

Prensky, M. (2001) *Digital Game-based Learning*. New York: McGraw-Hill.

Prensky, M. (2006) *'Don't Bother Me Mom – I'm Learning'*. St Paul, MN: Paragon House.

Pressley, M., Dolezal, S.E., Raphael, L.M., Mohan, L., Roehrig, A.D. & Bogner, K. (2003) *Motivating Primary-Grade Students*. New York: The Guilford Press.

Rogers, C. (1961) *On Becoming a Person*. Boston, MA: Houghton Mifflin.

Rosenberg, M. (1965) *Society and the Adolescent Self-image*. Princeton, NJ: Princeton University Press.

Rosenthal, R. & Jacobson, L. (1968) *Pygmalion in the Classroom: Teachers' Expectations and Pupils' Intellectual Development*. New York: Holt, Rinehart and Winston.

Rotter, J.B. (1954) *Social Learning and Clinical Psychology*. New York: Prentice-Hall.

Rudduck, J. (2003) *Consulting Pupils about Teaching and Learning*. Teaching and

Learning Research Briefing. Available at: www.tlrp.org/pub/documents/no5_ruddock.pdf

Ryan, R.M. & Deci, E.L. (2000) Self-determination theory and the facilitation of intrinsic motivation, self-development, and well-being. *American Psychologist*, 55 (1), 68–78.

Sassaroli, S. & Ruggiero, G.M. (2005) The role of stress in the association between low self-esteem, perfectionism, and worry, and eating disorders. *International Journal of Eating Disorders*, 37, 135–41.

Scottish Government (2009a) *Curriculum for Excellence. Religious and Moral Education: Principles and Practice*. Edinburgh: The Stationery Office. Available at: www.ltscotland.org.uk/learningteachingandassessment/curriculumareas/rme/nondenominational/principlesandpractice/index.asp

Scottish Government (2009b) *Curriculum for Excellence. Religious and Moral Education: Experiences and Outcomes*. Edinburgh: The Stationery Office. Available at: www.ltscotland.org.uk/learningteachingandassessment/curriculumareas/rme/nondenominational/eandos/index.asp

Seligman, M. (1995) *The Optimistic Child*. Boston, MA: Houghton Mifflin.

Shavelson, R.J., Hubner, J.J. & Stanton, G.C. (1976) Self-concept: validation of construct interpretations. *Review of Educational Research*, 46, 407–41.

Shulman, L.S. (1986) Those who understand: knowledge growth for teaching. *Educational Researcher*, 15, 4–14.

Shulman, L.S. (1987) Knowledge and teaching: foundations of the new reform, *Harvard Educational Review*, 57 (1), 1–22.

Smelser, N. (1989) Self-esteem and social problems: an introduction. In N.J.S.A.M. Mecca & J. Vasconcellos (eds) *The Social Importance of Self-esteem* (pp. 1–23). Berkeley, CA: University of California Press.

Smith, I. (1999) *Is Praise Always a Good Thing?* Dundee: SCCC.

Smith, R. (2002) Self-esteem: the kindly apocalypse. *Journal of Philosophy of Education*, 36 (1), 87–100.

Smith, R. (2004) *Creating the Effective Primary School: A Guide for School Leaders and Teachers*. London: Routledge.

Surgenor L.J., Maguire, S., Russell, J. & Touyz , S. (2006) Self-liking and self-competence: relationship to symptoms of anorexia nervosa. *European Eating Disorders Review*, 15 (2), 139–45.

Tafarodi, R.W., Marshall, T.C. & Milne, A.B. (2003) Self-esteem and memory. *Journal of Personality and Social Psychology*, 84, 29–45.

Tafarodi, R.W. & Milne, A.B. (2002) Decomposing global self-esteem. *Journal of Personality*, 70 (4), 443–83.

Tafarodi, R.W. & Swann, W.B. Jr. (1995) Self-liking and self-competence as dimensions of global self-esteem: initial validation of a measure. *Journal of Personality Assessment*, 65, 322–42.

Tanner, R.E.S. (2007) *Social Behaviour of Children*. New Delhi: Concept Publishing.

Thompson, T. & Hepburn, J. (2003) Causal uncertainty, claimed and behavioural self-handicapping. *British Journal of Educational Psychology*, 73, 247–66.

Thurston, A., Duran, D., Cunningham, E., Blanch, S. & Topping, K. (2009) International online reciprocal peer tutoring to promote modern language development in primary schools. *Computers & Education*, 53 (2), 462–72.

Topping, K.J. (2001a) *Peer Assisted Learning: A Practical Guide for Teachers.* Cambridge, MA: Brookline Books.

Topping, K.J. (2001b) *Thinking, Reading, Writing: A Practical Guide to Paired Learning with Peers, Parents and Volunteers.* London: Continuum.

Toynbee, P. (2001) At last we can abandon that tosh about low self-esteem. *The Guardian*, 28 December.

Twenge, J.M. & Campbell, W.K. (2009) *The Narcissism Epidemic: Living in the Age of Entitlement.* New York: Simon & Schuster.

Werner, E. & Smith, R. (1992) *Overcoming the Odds: High-risk Children from Birth to Adulthood.* New York: Cornell University Press.

Wetton, N. & Cansell, P. (1993) *Feeling Good: Raising Self-Esteem in the Primary School Classroom.* London: Forbes.

White, R. (1963) Ego and reality in psychoanalytic theory: a proposal regarding independent ego energies. *Psychological Issues*, 3, 125–50.

Winstanley, C. (2010) *The Ingredients of Challenge.* Stoke-on-Trent: Trentham Books.

Index